Monologues for Adults

**60 Original Monologues to
Stand Out, Inspire, and Shine**

Monologues for Adults

60 Original Monologues to Stand Out, Inspire, and Shine

Mike Kimmel
Foreword by Susannah Devereux

Copyright © 2021 Mike Kimmel

All rights reserved.

No portion of this book may be reproduced or transmitted in any form or by any means, electronic or mechanical, including photocopying, recording, or by any information storage or retrieval system, except for the inclusion of brief quotations in reviews.

ISBN 13: 9781953057068
Library of Congress Control Number 2021911161

Monologues for Adults:
60 Original Monologues to Stand Out, Inspire, and Shine
The Professional Actor Series: Book 2

Ben Rose Creative Arts
New York - Los Angeles

Publisher's Cataloging-in-Publication Data
provided by Five Rainbows Cataloging Services

Names: Kimmel, Mike, author. | Devereux, Susannah, writer of foreword.
Title: Monologues for adults : 60 original monologues to stand out, inspire, and shine / Mike Kimmel ; [foreword by] Susannah Devereux.
Description: Los Angeles : Ben Rose Creative Arts, 2021. | Series: Professional actor.
Identifiers: LCCN 2021911161 (print) | ISBN 978-1-953057-06-8 (paperback) | ISBN 978-1-953057-07-5 (ebook)
Subjects: LCSH: Monologues. | Acting--Auditions. | Method acting. | Acting--Study and teaching. | BISAC: PERFORMING ARTS / Monologues & Scenes. | PERFORMING ARTS / Acting & Auditioning.
Classification: LCC PN2080 .K56 2021 (print) | LCC PN2080 (ebook) | DDC 812/.6--dc23.

Interior design by Booknook.biz

Praise for
Monologues for Adults

"This is the only monologue book you'll ever need!!! Mike Kimmel shares a wonderful and vast selection of monologues designed for adults about the everyday issues in real life that everyone can relate to—with some interesting twists. Some are quite spiritual in nature. Mike has an interest in putting positivity out in the world on a daily basis and his depth shows in his writing. Instead of searching through plays, to find something right for your type, you will find what you're looking for right here and be able to tailor the monologue to you or the character you choose to play."

   ~ Jeri Slater
      Advertising Agency Executive Producer
      Saatchi & Saatchi, Publicis North America

"Mike Kimmel, brilliant yet again! This time he's created real life scenarios for both adult and young adult actors. I've read these scenarios and what Mike's stories do is make you think, and more than that, they make you feel, really feel. And isn't that where real acting occurs? When you feel your way through a scene you go deeper into your authentic self. You're not memorizing words from a page, you're expressing emotion from your core. Mastering that is the holy grail. Mike, thank you... what a gift, yet again!"

   ~ Suzanne Lyons
      Feature Film Producer, Snowfall Films
      Bailey's Billions, Time Toys, Séance, Portal,
      Undertaking Betty, Jericho Mansions, The Calling,
      The Heart Is Deceitful Above All Things, In My Life

"Very smart original writing for adult actors to keep their emotional and technical instrument ready for the work. Mike brings his own professional experience and knowledge as an actor and writer to the scripts to give great versatility for talent to work on. As a talent representative myself, seeing scripts and sides for auditions each day, Mike has hit the pulse of what actors would need to work on to bring their best foot forward when opportunities present themselves."

~ Myreon Arslan
Talent Agent and Owner,
MJB Talent Agency, Los Angeles, CA

"I've been an actor for more than 30 years, starting in L.A. in the late 80s. I have taught acting for the past 15 years, and monologues have always been at the core of my training. I use them nearly every day with beginning students and working professionals alike. Monologues can lead you to deeper subtext, interesting physicality, focus, and gravitas. Mike's monologues are some of the best I've ever seen as they afford each actor a fresh path to find complex layers making the scene their own. I'm excited to introduce them to all my students and see what we can discover together. Thank you, Mike, for the great work and a gift to every actor!"

~ Jim Blumetti
Actor and Acting Coach
Salem, In Plain Sight, Walker, Texas Ranger, The Good Guys, Bail Out, Stage 5, A Miracle for Haven, The Greg Ellis Show

"Mike Kimmel's books not only give you some fresh and new monologues for young actors to learn and perform, but the content is thought provoking and highly relatable. These pieces allow a performer to speak their words in a truthful manner which is a key first step any actor should hope to attain. Highly recommend."

> ~ Danny Arroyo
> Actor, Filmmaker, Producer, and Writer
> *Sangre Negra, African Mystique, Socio, Day Labor, Bite, Power, The Resistance, Nobody's Angel, The Detective, Predator: Concrete Jungle, Donna on the Go, 3rd Eye*

"As an acting coach, I am always looking for monologues with depth and space for the actor to examine interesting, important themes. The topics that Kimmel explores in this book provide rich material that is perfectly crafted for young adults to delve into. There are many thought-provoking characters to choose from, and each has a unique perspective that is worthy of studying and performing."

> ~ Misty Marshall
> Actor, Singer, and Songwriter
> Executive Director, Empowerment thru Arts LLC,
> Advisory Board Member and Lieutenant Governor,
> LA Music Commission, Sony recording artist
> and *American Idol* semi-finalist

"Mike Kimmel, in his book **Monologues for Adults**, makes everyday experiences come alive. His monologues are poetically written, giving performers an opportunity to create mood and meaning on stage."

~ Florene Villane
Associate Film Professor
MiraCosta College, Oceanside, California

"Mike's monologues are not only relevant but versatile. They allow each actor to make their own strong choices to bring a deeper, more truthful meaning to the words they are saying."

~ Sarah McLean
Actor, Producer, and Writer
Defending Jacob, 3 Strikes, Buddy Cops, One Rule,
Hip Hop Cabaret, Speed Therapy, ReAction, Dragonfly

"Mike's monologues are not only great for young actors to use in perfecting their craft and auditioning for roles, they also provide some valuable life lessons. They provide the readers with food for thought about real life situations and frustrations they may be encountering and serve as a form of inspiration. Every monologue provides a life lesson and balm for the soul. I highly recommended this book for young adults … actors or not!"

~ Tina Guillot
Public Speaker and Trainer
Toastmasters International
District 68 Director, 2017-2018

"A hearty volume of well thought out monologues. Nothing casual about them! Just long enough for the audience to be interested in you and short enough to keep them wanting more. My personal favorite is "When the World," as it reminds me of a scene out of a sports film, when the coach really lights up his team before a game. Motivational monologues by Mighty Mike Kimmel!"

~ GiGi Erneta
Actress, Radio and TV Host, and Writer
Flag of My Father, When the Bough Breaks, Roswell, New Mexico, VEEP, The Purge, Nashville, The First, Jane the Virgin, Risen, American Crime, Queen of the South, Scandal, NCIS New Orleans, Dallas, Friday Night Lights, Veronica Mars, Holiday in Santa Fe

"Wow! It is so refreshing to find such a generous compilation of wonderfully written monologues that incorporate such positivity and sincerity—for adults! An actor's life is not always the overnight-success-story we see in the movies. Don't get me wrong, success is real and it is achievable—but it takes effort and a lot of 'I'll never give up-ness.' What is that word? Determination! Our road is not always easy. In my opinion, these are more than monologues, they are the key to a powerful mindset that will help you push forward on your journey. As Mike says, 'When the world tells you to step back, do yourself a favor. Step forward.'"

~ Cait Brasel
Actor and Filmmaker
Distant Vision, Francis Ford Coppola's Live Cinema Workshop, Robot Riot, The Adventures of ARI, MONO, MONO Deux, My Robot Friend, Agnes, Wait!, Out of Exile

"With Mike Kimmel's monologues, I can feel confident in knowing I'll be performing an ear-catching piece that will engage the audience in an unexpected way. Not only does it take the actor through a journey of self-discovery, but the listener as well. At times, I found myself experiencing the sensation that Mike had taken my own thoughts and feelings and incorporated them into a monologue while providing valuable insight. It's as if you're getting a life lesson each time you read, study or perform one and, at times, can be transformational. His monologues are entertaining, honest, creative, and packed with inspiration that will definitely grab the listener's attention, which is usually half the battle. In addition to being excellent monologues, they're also great reading to help promote a daily positive mindset and outlook."

~ Gwendolynn Murphy
   Dallas Mavericks Dancers Alumni
   Theater, Film and TV Actress
   The Harrowing, Breakers, Murder Made Me Famous,
   Hiding in Plain Sight, No Ordinary Love, Blind Blood,
   The Witches of the Watch, Walker, Texas Ranger

For Sharon and Billy Mervis

"Your profession is not what brings home your weekly paycheck. Your profession is what you're put here on Earth to do, with such passion and such intensity that it becomes spiritual in nature."

~ Vincent Van Gogh

Contents

Praise for **Monologues for Adults**	v
Foreword	xix
Acknowledgments	xxiii
Introduction	xxv
The Story of Mom and Dad	1
When the World	2
The Beauty of No	3
Survival Jobs	4
In My Little Studio Apartment	5
The Ugly Sweatshirt	6
Looks Can Be Deceiving	7
Who I'm Supposed To Be	8
Your Unique Contribution	9
Make More Deposits	10
Welcome To My 2.0	11
Why Am I in a Bad Mood?	12
Positive People. Negative Thoughts.	13
Keep Building. Keep Believing.	14

A Million to One	15
When People Don't Care	16
It's Not Personal	17
Baby Steps	18
Well Done vs. Well Said	19
Do Something Better	20
Say Something Better	21
Yesterday	22
I Can. I Shall. I Must. I Do. And I Am.	23
Job or Career?	24
Walk into any Bookstore	25
The Fear Door	26
Try Something Different	27
Trying To Fit In	28
Money and Happiness	29
Random Acts of Coffee	30
The Great Protector	31
The Flat Earther	32
The Big Lie	33
Twenty Minutes	34
Wait Thirty Minutes	35
Bird Watching	36

Monologues for Adults

The People Watcher	37
The DNA Test	38
I Bought a Vintage Car	39
How Do We Decide?	40
First, Last, and Only	41
Good Bad Role Models	42
The Statute of Limitations	43
Email Etiquette	44
About Fifty Percent	46
Exercising in the Park	48
The Squirrels' Revenge	50
My Blind Date	52
Autonomy	54
When the Smoke Clears	56
Visiting Aunt Cathy	58
Anatomy of a Compliment	60
The Honor of Disrespect	62
An Inconvenient Convenience	64
On the Backs of Envelopes	66
Fifty-Two Bad Ones	68
Pie in the Sky	70
He Begged Me Not To Go	72

Mike Kimmel

The Rocky Marciano Technique	74
An Older Driver	76
Afterword	77
Help Spread The Word	79
Recommended Reading	81
About Susannah Devereux	84
About Mike Kimmel	86

Foreword

Wow. I asked "Mighty Mike" Kimmel for this book and I got it! I'll explain in a bit, but as much as I may want to pretend he wrote this book just for me, ***Monologues for Adults*** is more than just a gem for any and every adult actor, it is destined to become a *gold standard* in the adult actor toolbox.

The stories that will come forth over the years proclaiming how this unassuming little book empowered actors all around the world will fill a giant book of its own. I predict ***Monologues for Adults*** will be highly recommended by acting coaches, agents and managers around the world for as long as actors are auditioning. I'm sure you'll agree once you hear my Mighty Mike Kimmel story.

Ready for the ride? That's how it started … I needed a ride, and what I got was a life-long friend, Mike Kimmel, one of the dearest, most talented, hard working, honest, caring and deserving souls I've met in my extensive journey. Ask the length of that journey at your own peril.

The first thing you need to know is, I'm a Kiwi actress, that means I'm from New Zealand, and some twenty-four years ago, I landed in the glorious city of Los Angeles destined for Hollywood to study with U.S. acting coach Jeremy Comey, whom I'd met at an acting workshop the New Zealand Film Commission had set up for actors, writers and directors.

I had just finished four years on the #1 New Zealand TV show ***Shortland Street***, a cross between ***ER*** and ***General Hospital***, playing the recurring role of Diane Neilson and a commercial contract playing the Mom in a series of commercials for **Noel Leeming**, a leading technology and appliance retailer. Interestingly, **Shortland Street** is still running and is the fastest turn around television production in the world.

I was fresh off the boat and I'd gone to a casting director workshop that was "in the Valley" some distance from where I was staying. At the time, I was taking public transport to workshops, meetings and auditions. Public transportation in Los Angeles is quite different from N.Z., so I was hoping *not* to use that for my long return trip.

At the end of the workshop, very determined, I asked at the top of my lungs, "Is anyone going back to Hollywood, I need a ride please!" and the perfect gentleman that is Mike Kimmel answered, "I'll take you." So was the beginning of a long and wonderful friendship.

We were immediate friends, have been now for twenty-four years. That's part of why I had the honor to get advance copies of his previous books to review and give him deserving accolades. In his book of this series, **Monologues for Teens**, I was so utterly impressed with what he'd created and its value to young actors, in my review I'd asked, "Please write some for adults!"

He did. Here it is, **Monologues for Adults**, it's clear, it's intelligent, it's logical, it's diverse, you can literally find whatever you need in what I call a manual of malleable personalities, it's utterly empowering to have these in your arsenal, and there's a very common sense "technical/psychological" reason for using these over other established monologues. I totally believe this book could give you an extra edge and a huge confidence booster, and no actor should be without a copy of **Monologues for Adults**. Here's why.

How many times have you asked your fellow actors, classmates and friends in the business, "Can you suggest a monologue for me, I have an agent meeting or audition?"

Ah! The art of finding the perfect showcase monologue—is it an art or a slippery slope slanted toward the waters of lost auditions? I say Splash! You can decide for yourself.

If I was going to be fancy, I'd call this my Theory of Diminishing Attention, but it's really just common sense. When I give an audition, I want to have the attention on me, all of it, on my delivery, on my words, on me, 100 percent. If I'm giving a monologue that's been immortalized by some Oscar/Tony winning actor who originated it, and then later given by a zillion actors auditioning with it, then here's what happens, it cannot logically be otherwise.

The listener cannot help but refer mentally to the original and compare word by word, it's impossible *not* to do so. Almost by default, their brain will automatically and instinctively be mentally comparing every single word to see if they were given correctly. They will also have focus on how the original was delivered emotionally for comparison. All that is huge "lost" attention, attention on comparison that I want on ME. I want them to hear my every word and nuance without attention anywhere else, to see and hear me. That makes good sense in my world.

Using a Mighty Mike monologue, 100 percent of the attention is on me and my words and my delivery. AND, because the listener doesn't know what's coming, they have to pay extra close attention to engage my content! They must be right there in the moment and really hear *me*, and feel my emotion, and this *present time connection* makes me real to them, not a machine spewing someone else's famous words, in that moment they see *me!*

And a well given, uniquely crafted monologue is *memorable*.

How does an actor develop a set of razor sharp, unique and memorable monologues? It all starts with a manual chock-full of multi-faceted, emotionally layered monologues of every type for any occasion, diverse with wit and emotion, ready to be shaped into your own style, and always unique and memorable.

Problem solved, **Monologues for Adults**. Unique and memorable, what else can I say? If that's what you want, you'll find the monologues you need in this book to make them your own and maybe change your career. Dig in, stretch your mind with them and find three or four monologues for your toolbox.

Who knows, one confidently given monologue, listened to with full attention and not compared to anyone else, may reveal you in such a way that you are cast for the part of a lifetime, just like that.

Honor your craft, honor yourself, get this book, have fun and deliver well.

I asked for this book and I have received. I certainly hope you find the same empowerment from this deep, purposeful and masterful work of art. I'm so proud to call him my friend and be a small part of this.

Mighty Mike, thanks for the ride!

Susannah Devereux
Nashville, Tennessee

Acknowledgments

As always, a million thanks to Mollie, Adele, and Tammy, my three wonderful sisters. Their kindness and generosity are legendary—and are very much appreciated.

Many thanks to Kimberly Bliquez, GiGi Erneta, Karen, Katharine, and Jennifer Kramer, Suzanne Lyons, Misty Marshall, Gwendolynn Murphy, Karen Pavlick, Jeri Slater, Danny Arroyo, Myron Arslan, Erik Beelman, Jim Blumetti, Stephen Bowling, David Breland, Francis Ford Coppola, Chuck Disney, Gene LeBell, Morgan Roberts, Ben Rose, Will Wallace, and William Wellman Jr. for all their encouragement, support, and expert advice.

Very special thanks to Susannah "Devastating" Devereux, for sharing her powerful, highly personal story in the foreword to this book. Susannah is a dear friend and one of the smartest, strongest, most capable actors I've met in this industry. She's one of the kindest and most gracious, as well. I am grateful for our many years of friendship and camaraderie, and look forward to many more collaborations in the years ahead.

Introduction

Thank you for selecting this book. I hope **Monologues for Adults** will be a valuable tool to guide, support, and encourage you through all your auditions, rehearsals, performances—and your entire long-term actor journey. I hope this book will become a go-to resource for adult actors—and help you safely navigate the puzzling, inconsistent, and unforgiving waters of the entertainment industry.

I've been in show business for a long time—not only as an actor, but also in a variety of roles behind the scenes. One of the benefits of working and teaching in the entertainment industry for many years is the opportunity to observe the repetition of plans, events, and outcomes. Repetition allows us to recognize patterns of action and behavior that reveal themselves to be consistent. I believe the search for consistent patterns always leads us directly to the truth.

A Challenge for Actors

It's rare to hear a monologue with any sort of uplifting or encouraging message. Many actors make the mistake of selecting monologues with mean-spirited, sarcastic, inflammatory, inappropriate, disrespectful, and even violent overtones and subtext. Many are dark, depressing, pessimistic, and overly argumentative. Many actors, sorry to say, also carry a black cloud of gloom and negativity with them everywhere they go. This is a common trap for actors. Maybe it's a fondness for edgy material. Maybe it's an obsession with injecting "conflict" into every script. Maybe it's a too-literal interpretation of the question, "What am I fighting for?" Maybe it's a fundamental misunderstanding of the dual role (more about this later) that actors are meant to play in the larger production. Maybe it's all of the above.

However, when we put ourselves in the shoes of a casting director who must listen to monologues all day long, we can see that this is not the most effective approach. It's much wiser to present yourself differently—as the single bright spot in an overcrowded field on a dark and gloomy day. As actors, we must train our minds to think like producers and directors, not like other actors. Would you want to invite a walking black cloud of gloom, pessimism, and negativity into a production you've been developing for years—a project that puts your professional reputation (and millions of dollars) at stake? Probably not.

A Solution for Actors

One of the best ways to create rapport and build connection with industry professionals is through your work—and your choice of material. An actor's choice of material is an important first hurdle to overcome in the casting process. It's a subtle personality test, giving producers and directors an indication of how that actor truly sees the world. It's their first clue about how that actor will perform on set. Make the decision, therefore, to audition with a monologue that offers an uplifting, thought-provoking, and outer-directed message.

The monologues in this collection embody real life characters and situations—and are intended to inspire, encourage, and offer food for thought between the written lines. They are clean, gender-neutral, and appropriate for all audiences. If you can deliver a positive message or life lesson as subtext, while telling a compelling story in a conversational, realistic manner, you will be light years ahead of the curve. You'll be well on your way to standing out, shining, and drawing attention to yourself in a positive, insightful manner. This choice indicates to producers and directors that you understand the role of the actor relative to their production as a whole. You're demonstrating that you bring something valuable to the negotiation table—and can offer a mutually beneficial working relationship to those in a position to hire you.

This is a skill set like any other, and is well worth developing. It's a subtle shift in attitude that is extremely powerful. This is a difficult concept for many actors, however, and is closely related to what I call, "The Dirty Little Secret of Show Business."

The Dirty Little Secret of Show Business

Here it is: Producers and directors are never really sure the project they're creating—and we're auditioning for—is going to work. There are thousands of hidden surprises that can pop up unexpectedly and throw a monkey wrench into the best-laid plans of every production. Even with an excellent script and cast, there is rarely a guarantee of success. I call this the dirty little secret of our industry because nobody ever talks about it. Nobody talks about it because nobody takes the time to think like a producer.

Because so many things can go wrong on stage and screen, producers and directors try to minimize their risk by hiring the same actors (and crew members) again and again. This is true even at the star level. Why does Martin Scorsese, for example, cast Robert DeNiro so frequently? He's a brilliant actor, of course. That's a given, but it's not the complete story. Mr. Scorsese has his pick of brilliant actors and A-list talent on every project he directs. He continues to select Mr. DeNiro through the years because he knows he'll have an outstanding working relationship—and no surprises—with his star on set. That comfortable, consistent, effective working relationship is incredibly important for directors and producers. It's the actor's job to convince directors and producers—through subtle communication in our performances—that they can begin to develop that same level of trust with us.

My Own Experiences and Discoveries

For more than twenty years, I've been blessed with opportunities to work in scripted and improvisational theater, film, television, commercials, commercial print, hosting, voice-overs, corporate training films, music videos, theater and film festivals, and emerging media. I started in New York, made the move to Los Angeles, and also found work in a dozen smaller markets throughout the United States. I've worked on the other side of the camera in a variety of production roles too, allowing me to view the industry from the perspective of our producers, directors, casting directors, talent agents, and managers. These experiences have offered a clear picture of the industry and its many interrelated moving parts.

You may not recognize my name and face, but I've had the experience of going out on thousands of auditions and booking hundreds of jobs through dozens of agents and casting directors on both U.S. coasts and many states in between. The result has been twenty-plus years of unofficial—but practical—hands-on research through classes, workshops, open calls, auditions, meetings, interviews, collaborations, rehearsals, performances, wrap parties, red carpet premieres, and all manner of industry events. My laboratory has always been the real world. My experiments have yielded wonderful successes and crushing disappointments. Through it all, I've realized that my own results can benefit my fellow travelers on this same worthy path.

Since 2014, it's been a personal goal to help simplify and demystify the entertainment industry by writing a series of contemporary, gender-neutral, family-friendly scene and monologue books for actors of all ages. The big picture goal has always been to help newcomers find their own effective starting points in the performing arts. I also hope to give something back to an industry that has been very good to me through the years.

Real World Advice from the Trenches

Though the advice I offer is just my own opinion, it's an opinion based upon things I've actually observed and experienced firsthand. Additionally, I have a small circle of friends and colleagues with solid credits and background in all facets of the industry. We ask one another for advice whenever a challenging situation arises. A typical conversation begins with, "Okay, I guarantee you've never heard THIS ONE before." The collaboration and communication is helpful for each of us. Together, we all gain a greater understanding of the industry and its many complexities. Several of these close friends and associates—like Susannah Devereux—have been gracious enough to lend their knowledge and expertise to this book series, as well. In the entertainment industry, it's extremely important to surround yourself with creative, capable, competent people whose opinions and ethical standards you can trust. One thing we all have in common is that we're far more interested in real world application than classroom theory.

The Human Connection

An important, often overlooked, aspect of acting is psychology, the study of the wonderfully complex human mind. We must remember the human element in every industry interaction. We're in a people business. There's a tendency for actors to lose sight of the fact that the directors, producers, agents, and casting directors we audition for are human beings first and foremost. They were human beings long before they ever broke into the entertainment industry. They step into the audition rooms with their own unique backgrounds, personalities, and challenges—just like actors do.

This reminder seems obvious but is worth reinforcing again and again. Concentrating on the human connection helps us avoid appearing needy and desperate inside the audition room. Actors can become so focused on our own needs—the desire to be liked, the desire to be hired, the desire for positive feedback and approval—that we fail to consider the needs of the folks we're reading for. This is understandable. There's a great deal of pressure to perform at our best on audition day. Additionally, monologue auditions tend to be far more stressful than multi-character scene auditions. We're all alone up there. We shine or sink by our individual efforts. Unfortunately, I've seen this combination of pressures drive actors to become inner-directed—and lose their broader frame of reference with regard to the project as a whole. Ultimately, this narrow focus contributes to a stereotype of actors as shallow, egotistical, narcissistic, and painfully self-involved.

Shifting Your Focus

Actors who can shift focus outside themselves—and their own desire to get the job—are far more likely to be seen as effective team players. This is not easy to do. Actors must walk a fine line, representing themselves as reliable members of a team, while still shining brightly as individualists. Why is this important? Because even though we perform solo work with our monologues, we must simultaneously keep the big picture in mind. Once hired, the actor becomes part of a much larger ensemble production, collaborating with many other industry professionals in a wide range of separate, highly specialized fields.

I agree wholeheartedly with what Susannah Devereux explains in her wonderful foreword to this book. Actors must do everything in their power to capture the full attention of the powers that be. We want all eyes on us, front and center, and with no distractions. We must be authentic, unique, strong, dynamic, and memorable. At the same time, we must indirectly convey the impression that, once hired, we'll be indispensable additions to the team—helping to ensure a successful production for our producers and directors on set. Actors who can train themselves to subtly communicate their understanding of an actor's dual role in the production can increase their opportunities dramatically—and connect with producers and directors in a far more effective manner.

This amounts to a subtle shift in intent and is well worth exploring for long-term success. Actors who can learn to present themselves as effective and conscientious team players are also likely to be seen as problem solvers—rather than problem creators. We've all been around problem creators, chaotic people who carry a great deal of personal baggage with them from day to day and from job to job. Show business seems to have more than its fair share of talented people who, unfortunately, simply cannot get out of their own way. They are their own worst enemies. Through the years, I've seen so many talented actors burn bridges, self-destruct, and obliterate future opportunities for themselves and those around them. Has this been your experience? I'm embarrassed to admit it, but I've made some classic blunders in my own career, as well. Moving forward, however, we can analyze our actions, recognize the patterns, and develop new strategies to help us make better decisions in the future.

I can promise you that the last thing directors and producers want is to bring a problematic actor into the fold. There's far too much at stake. Therefore, we must focus on becoming problem solvers rather than problem creators. This is a valuable exercise in mental gymnastics because it trains us to think the way producers and directors think. Producers and directors are the ones who can hire actors, so it's important for us to understand the psychology at work on their side of the negotiation table. Every audition and booking is a complex negotiation. This is equally true for stage and screen roles. The industry professionals we audition for are trained to analyze each new project in terms of the potential problems that may eventually derail it. They look at every step in their long, grueling production process and try to predict problems that may arise—the difficulties that can sabotage them, and the challenges they can more easily avoid through relevant prior experience.

Check Your Baggage

Finally, please understand that experienced industry professionals can smell desperation, narcissism, nihilism, and chaos the moment they slither into the audition room. Never allow these career-killing attitudes to attach themselves to you. Always check your baggage at the door. Make it a habit to continually self-monitor. Keep a close watch on how you're presenting yourself to others. Make sure to keep the drama on the page and on the stage—and out of your life.

It's truly empowering to walk into an audition—and onto a set after booking the role—with the attitude that you're a problem solver. You are there to help the production move forward seamlessly, ahead of schedule, and under budget. Hiring you will save the production time and money. You're not just another self-involved actor trying to add a new line to your resume, a new clip to your reel, and a new deposit to your bank account. This is precisely the mindset we should carry with us into every meeting and audition. It's a powerful, outer-directed mindset that will set you apart from all the other actors auditioning for your role.

If you're new to the business, guard and maintain your optimism and idealism. If you've been acting for a long time and feel yourself starting to become jaded and cynical, then keep reminding yourself why you became an actor in the first place. It's always helpful to get back to the basics, even if you've been acting for a decade or more. Author and business trainer Denis Waitley said it best: "Chase your passion, not your pension."

I hope the monologues in this book resonate with you and your audiences. I am confident that they will work well for actors of all ages and physical types in the audition room—and help you stand out, inspire, and shine. My most fervent wish for actors is that these monologues—and the ideas presented in the foreword and introduction—will bring you several steps closer to reaching and surpassing all your goals in work and in life.

Keep reminding yourself that if a favorite actor has accomplished something you admire, then you have the potential to do equally well. Their accomplishments are tangible proof that those same goals are accessible to all of us. Maybe you will achieve even greater things in your own life and career. It all starts with training yourself to become a problem solver. It all starts with learning to think like a producer and director. Actors who can present themselves as problem solvers—and then deliver the goods—are worth their weight in vibranium. Always strive to become a problem solver, because every project we audition for (and book) will have more than its own fair share of problems to be overcome.

Stay strong, stay smart, and stay focused. I wish you the very best of happiness and success on this worthy path and wild adventure.

Mike Kimmel
Los Angeles, California

The Story of Mom and Dad

Mom and Dad were happy for twenty-five years. Then they met.

It was pretty much all over after that. There was a strong animal attraction, apparently. That's where I came from.

But they just weren't good for each other. And all that chemistry doesn't mean much when two people have nothing to talk about over their morning coffee.

And I think that's a crying shame. But not so unusual at all. I believe there's more divorces than happily ever afters nowadays. Over fifty percent. Wild, right? Seventy-five percent in California where my folks met. Let that percolate in your minds a little while, will you? That calculates out to a seventy-five percent failure rate. You can do better than that in Vegas. Rolling the dice. Which I suppose is what my parents did.

My dad got custody of the car. My mom got custody of me. I'd like to think she got the better of that settlement.

I still see Mom and Dad every week or two. Separately, of course. They won't see each other. But I have a good relationship with both of them. We have long talks. As an adult, I've gotten to know both my parents real well. And I understand them much better now than I did years ago.

Maybe that's why I'm still single.

When the World

When the world tells you to step back, do yourself a favor. Step forward.

When the world tells you to step down, step up.

When the world tells you to go away ... we don't need you, we don't want you ... grit your teeth and show up just one more time.

When the world knocks you down a hundred fifty-seven times, you get back up a hundred fifty-eight times.

When the world tells you to back up, pack up, and give up ... tell the world to shut up. Because you're supposed to be here. You belong here. When the world tells you, "No," you tell yourself, "Yes."

When the world gives you a million reasons why nothing's ever going to work out right for you ... train your mind to forget all the reasons it won't work ... and believe strongly in the one reason that it will. Because there are people ... people you haven't even met yet ... who are already connected to your destiny.

So when it feels like nobody in the whole world believes in you, that's when it's most important to believe in yourself. Become the hero in your own life story. Become the person you needed most when you were young.

Because one day you're going to thank yourself for never giving up on yourself. And one day you're going to thank me for reminding you just how brilliant, powerful, and unstoppable you are—no matter what this big, bad, beautiful world tells you.

The Beauty of No

I've got no news for you. No, no, it's not that I don't have "any" news for you. Quite the opposite. I have very important, highly specific news to share about my favorite word, "no."

Because sometimes in life, no matter what you do ... or fail to do ... the answer is "no" before you even walk through the door.

No, you didn't get that job you wanted. No, that person you were interested in wasn't interested back. No, that new car just had one too many zeros in the price tag.

I've found that no is a great teacher. No teaches us clarity, humility, and perseverance. No teaches us to live within our means, stay focused on the things that are really important in life, and not waste time chasing after every shiny new object that flashes in front of our eyes.

No teaches us we don't need every new thing we want ... or, honestly, that the world tells us we want. We may want them, but we don't need them. Some things we can live without. No teaches us how strong, capable, and resilient we are without those things. This may not be the lesson we want, but sometimes it's exactly the lesson we need. That's why "no" is my favorite word.

And, no, I won't be angry if it becomes your favorite new word too. No is big enough for all of us to share.

Survival Jobs

I have a confession to make. I've bounced around from job to job. Guess I've done that most of my life. Ever since I got out of college, to tell you the truth. Didn't ever stick with any one job too long, … because none of them were really what I wanted to do. My Uncle Jake calls them "survival jobs."

They're jobs that keep me going while I'm grinding away and pursuing my music. Because music is what I really want to do most of all in this world. Making music is my major, definite purpose in life. But these other jobs bring in a … somewhat steady paycheck. They sure do. They help me keep my head above water so I'm not stressing too much between music opportunities.

And I'm incredibly grateful for every one of those jobs, believe me. Even though they're a real mixed bag of nuts. Catering. Waitering. Dishwasher. Busboy … uh, bus-person. Substitute teacher. Taxi driver. Forklift driver. Airport shuttle bus driver. Sign painter. Security guard. Bartender. Night watchman. Babysitter.

Wanna judge me? Go right ahead. Be my ghost. Tell me how I have no business waiting tables with a college degree. Heard it all before. Been there, done that, got the T-shirt. Doesn't matter what anybody else thinks about my jobs or my choices … or the way I'm living my life.

Because I am the world's greatest living expert on me. Those jobs pay the bills and are flexible … so I can keep making music. Right now, I have to do them. And I'm gonna keep doing what I have to do … so that someday I can do what I want to do.

In My Little Studio Apartment

I'm an artist. Not a famous one ... not yet, anyway. But who knows? With a little luck—and a lot of grit, spit, and tenacity, anything's possible. The sky's the limit. My work may show in a high-end gallery. Maybe even a museum. Why not? Other artists do it. Why not me?

I paint. I draw. I do watercolors, charcoals, sculpture. Even a little photography here and there. Pretty much anything and everything you can imagine—and some things you can't imagine—in the Visual Arts.

And I do it all out of my little studio apartment. Teeny, tiny little place ... but it serves its purpose ... and it serves me well.

Three hundred fifty square feet ... and I use every square inch of it. My easel doubles as a clothes dryer. My little folding television tray is my kitchen table, writing desk, and sculpture stand. And I mix my watercolors and paints in a little plastic basin from the dollar store. It fits perfectly inside my bathroom sink.

You should see my perfect little studio apartment. My beautiful little combination art studio and living space. Well, I guess you can't see it. The place isn't exactly big enough to have guests over. But I can take a photo ... or draw you a sketch to show you how it looks.

And I can do both those things pretty well, by the way. From all the hours and hours and hours of practice ... inside my little studio apartment.

The Ugly Sweatshirt

It was the ugliest sweatshirt I ever saw. It may have been the ugliest sweatshirt anybody ever saw. Nobody in their right mind would have ever chosen that sweatshirt. Way too ugly. In fact, if I hadn't taken it off the rack to try on … it probably would have stayed there for a year or more.

But trying it on revealed something to me. That was not only the ugliest sweatshirt on the planet … but also the most comfortable. Maybe the most comfortable garment I've ever worn.

So then it became an ethical dilemma. Do I buy it because it's comfortable, or do I leave it because it's ugly? There were plenty of compelling arguments on both sides of that negotiation, believe me.

But most compelling of all is the desire to be me … and not follow the herd mentality in all I say and do and am. And I'm happy to report I'm now the proud owner of an incredibly comfortable, astonishingly ugly sweatshirt.

And that purchase decision reminded me once more … never to live my life for other people. I've gotta be me.

Looks Can Be Deceiving

Don't believe everything you see. Looks can be deceiving. Salt looks just like sugar.

And the world is full of monsters with friendly faces. This world is also full of angels with beautiful souls ... covered head to toe with scars. Scars on the outside. The outside won't necessarily show you what's happening underneath the surface. Looks can be deceiving. Obi-Wan said it best. "Your eyes can deceive you, Luke. Don't trust them."

Good advice for you, me, and everyone else on this planet who thinks with their heart instead of their head. Think twice before you put your trust in someone. Don't judge a book by its cover. Trust is fine, but trusting in a person who's *earned* your trust is a whole lot smarter. Much better strategy.

And ... by the way ... people don't earn our trust just by being cute. Try to dig a little deeper than what's on the surface whenever you can. And here's a hint: You always can.

Doesn't matter if you've been fooled a million times in the past. You can change your pattern today. You can change everything in your ancient history. Trust me. You don't have to cling to all the old mistakes you made ... just because you spent so many years making them.

Mike Kimmel

Who I'm Supposed To Be

Sometimes I think I came from another planet. Other times I'm sure of it.

I'm not trying to be weird ... and freak you out. I guess I just don't think like everybody else. That's not a bad thing. That's a good thing.

Because I've gotta be me. I'm not supposed to be other people ... and other people are not supposed to be me. Especially when I see the way some people behave out there in the big, beautiful world.

I feel like I don't quite fit in. And don't really wanna fit in. I'm not on board with the way people put each other down, make rude, negative comments all day long, break the rules, lie, steal, cheat, cut each other off in traffic, throw their trash everywhere ... and all the other things people do when they're not functioning at their best.

And I'm not a goody two shoes. Far from it. Maybe a goody one shoe, because I know I'm not perfect. But I'm pretty happy and comfortable inside my own skin.

And that's a good thing because I'm the one who's gotta live there. Not other people. How about you? Do you remember who you were before the world told you who you were supposed to be ... where you're supposed to live ... what you're supposed to drive ... and how you're supposed to act?

I hope you do. Because I want to make friends with you. Not with the person everyone else tells you to be.

Your Unique Contribution

I have a confession to make. As I've gotten older, I always thought I would develop more patience and understanding with people. Thought I'd finally develop the emotional maturity to accept people as they are—warts and all.

And I do. I usually do. Until I reach the point when I don't.

That's my confession. I'm developing less and less patience with people who have zero patience with themselves. Or anyone else.

Narcissists. The Instant Gratification Crowd. The Slothful Sluggards. Give me. Get me. Buy me. Take me. People who think the world owes them a living.

Well, hate to break it to you, folks, but life owes us nothing. In fact, exactly the opposite is true. It is we—you and me—who owe everything to life. We're supposed to put in more than we take out.

Because, when you get right down to it, we owe life everything we've got. All the creativity, focus, and positive energy that came fully installed into our DNA at birth. Or our moments of creation.

Figure out what you can do better than everybody else on this planet and then go do it. Crush it. Do that thing like there's no tomorrow. Make your unique contribution on this beautiful blue marble in space that we all call home. After all, what else are we here for?

Make More Deposits

Stanford University did a study. Yeah, yeah, I know, they're always doing some kind of study. But this was a good one. This was important. They found that only eight percent of people are happy with their lives. Eight.

And one hundred percent of the people I know are not happy with that study.

Because that's some kind of crazy result!

But I think it comes down to this: Are you a giver or a taker in life? Most people are both. Nobody's one hundred percent. We're not robots. And we can't really expect to enjoy our lives one hundred percent either. But I think we can aim for quite a bit higher than Stanford University's eight percent.

So let me ask you. Which do you do more often—ask for help ... or offer it?

It's like going to the bank. Sometimes we make deposits. Sometimes we make withdrawals. My advice? Make more deposits than withdrawals.

Get in the habit of giving a little more of yourself. Put more back into the world than you take out. Be more of a giver than a taker. We may never become one hundred percenters ... but I know we can do a whole lot better than eight percent.

Welcome To My 2.0

Gossip. Jealousy. Back-biting. Sarcasm. Mockery.

Man, is that a lot of work! Just to maintain all that drama. I don't know how some people have the time. I guess they make the time. Gotta make time for the things that are most important to you in life.

Personally, I've got no time for all that mess. I am not even remotely interested in participating. Not interested in comparing myself to others, tearing anyone down, or talking behind their backs. It's a full-time job just keeping my own side of the street clean.

But it was not always that way. I used to be grumpy, sarcastic ... and a little bit mean. Honestly, though, I don't even recognize the old me anymore. Except when I see myself reflected in other people I'd like to avoid.

So what do you do when someone notices ... and points it out to you? Someone you've known a long time may say, "Hey! You've changed."

That's a good thing. Acknowledge the growth. Tell them, "Yes, I've changed. I've recently upgraded my version. This is the new me. Welcome to my 2.0."

Mike Kimmel

Why Am I in a Bad Mood?

Yesterday, I was in a bad mood. A guy at my job was really rude to me … and I was in a bad mood all day.

Then we had a lesson about that in my psychology class. Pretty good class. My professor explained it for us. She said it's like this. Imagine you have a big pile of money. About $86,400. That's a lot. Now imagine some mean creepo comes along and steals ten dollars from you. That's not good. But would you get so mad at that rude person that you spend the remaining $86,390 that's left in the pile … to try and get revenge on them for stealing that first ten dollars?

No, of course you wouldn't. I hope you wouldn't. You'd get on with your life. My psychology professor said we have 86,400 seconds in every day. So we shouldn't let 10 seconds of somebody's bad manners mess up the remaining 86,390 good seconds left in our day.

Think about that next time you're in a bad mood. Maybe someone else put you in a bad mood, but you can pull yourself out of it.

Try to remember the good part that's left in your day … and don't waste another precious minute trying to get back at someone who doesn't appreciate all the wonderful things you have to offer.

Positive People. Negative Thoughts.

People ask me how do I manage to stay so positive. Especially on those days when it looks like things aren't looking so good. Well, can I tell you a secret? Positive people also have negative thoughts. They just don't allow those thoughts to grow and destroy them.

My attitude is that I can't control how things look on the outside, but I can definitely control how I react on the inside. And my actions on the outside are a reflection of how I choose to think on the inside.

Because we always have a choice.

Just because you think something doesn't mean you have to let that thought run rampant all through your head ... and all through your day. You can choose a different choice.

That sure beats what most of my friends and family do ... which is gripe and complain about people who did them wrong ten years ago.

So my advice to me, you, and everybody else on this planet is to stay safe, stay strong, and stay positive.

And always remember—you don't have to believe every negative thought you think.

Keep Building. Keep Believing.

Do you remember the story of Noah and the Ark? I think everybody knows that one. Even if they never read one page of the Bible.

Well, just imagine Noah's friends and neighbors. They all must have thought old Noah was crazy. Building this giant boat in his back yard. Telling everybody the flood was coming. The neighbors probably called Noah a conspiracy theorist.

Then it started to rain.

Then Noah didn't look so crazy anymore.

Here's the takeaway. Noah didn't stop building the Ark to explain himself to every doubter, mocker, and hater who tried to rain on his parade.

Keep building whatever it is you want to create for yourself and your future. And your life. Let's all be more like Noah. Let's all keep working silently and steadily.

And what should you do when people start to gossip, call you crazy … or call you a conspiracy theorist?

Let the rain do the talking for you. The evidence will silence all those negative voices. The rain will wash away the judgement of your critics.

A Million to One

Did anyone ever tell you to forget it? Tell you that something you wanna do is too hard? Maybe that none of your plans, hopes, dreams, and goals are realistic?

Well, I'd like to offer you some very different advice. I'm here to encourage you in exactly the opposite direction.

I want you to forget all the people who try to rain on your parade. Forget everyone who tells you to forget it. Because those people have no idea what you're capable of. They're not you. They're giving you negative marks based upon their own assessment of how they see themselves. That's them—and has nothing whatsoever to do with you.

Bottom line is that you are the world's greatest living expert on yourself. So forget all the reasons your plan won't work and concentrate on the one reason that it will. Train yourself to believe thoroughly in that one reason.

And when people tell you the odds are a million to one?

That's fine. Be the one.

When People Don't Care

Here's some good advice, free of charge.

When people treat you like they don't care … believe them. Don't chase after them, either. Most importantly, don't follow their example. Make sure you don't treat yourself that same "I don't care" way too.

Because you've gotta be you. You've gotta be the real you. You're an original. There's only one of you out there in this big, beautiful world, and you've gotta be the real one. And everyone knows that an original is much more valuable than a copy. So always be true to you … and always try to create the best possible version of yourself that you can create.

You need you at one hundred percent. No matter how those people who don't treat you right may see you … or not see you. Trust me, you need you a whole lot more than you will ever need them.

So don't be too concerned about how people treat you.

Be very concerned about how you treat you.

It's Not Personal

Did you ever feel disrespected? Like people don't treat you as well as they treat other people?

Well, let me explain something for you. It's not personal. It's not really about you at all. It only happens to be directed your way when you happen to step into their malicious line of fire. It's really a reflection on them … and how they see the world … and how they see themselves.

Because most people don't even respect themselves. So how can they respect you?

They can't. And we should learn to appreciate their disrespect.

The disrespect of disreputable people is the single greatest compliment we can ever hope to receive. It's proof that we're not like them and don't fit into their disrespectful world view. Look at it like a stamp of approval that you can be proud of wearing. Disrespectful people don't see you as one of them. You're not a kindred spirit. You don't behave as abominably as they do … and that's definitely something you can be proud of.

Baby Steps

Little steps. Incremental steps. Baby steps. They're important because they all add up.

Martin Luther King talked about this. Way before my time, obviously, but he said, that we don't have to see the top step of the staircase. All we have to do is take the first step and set our sights upon the next step.

Sounds nice, but how can we apply it? Good question. With exercise, it's easy. We can always do a couple more reps. We can always do another set. We can always do an extra workout.

And it's easy with your job—and with school too. At work, you can show up earlier, stay later, and work a little harder. Not even a lot. Just a little. If you're in school, it's the same with homework. A little extra studying every day. A little more than is required. A little more than is assigned. Before you know it, you're a chapter ahead. Then two chapters ahead.

Baby steps help more than you think. Because most people take no steps. Zero forward motion. That's a guaranteed way to stay where you are. Where nothing's happening for you. Baby steps can take you right out of that "nothing's happening" neighborhood … and move you up the street to someplace a little more active. You just have to start. Starting is mandatory. You don't have to be great to start, but you do have to start to be great.

Well Done vs. Well Said

Ben Franklin said, "Well done is better than well said." We all need to up our game.

People say a lot, so I watch what they do. You are what you do, not what you say you'll do. And the difference between who you are and who you want to be ... or who you say you want to be ... is what you do.

So keep your promises to people ... and keep your promises to yourself ... and do what you say you're gonna do. Because a year from now, you're going to wish you started today.

And don't worry if people don't believe in you. Most people don't even believe in themselves. Besides, you need you more than you need them, trust me. So evaluate the people in your life around you. Then promote, demote, or terminate them as you see fit. You're the President and CEO of your life.

That's why it's so important to take the time to get to know yourself inside and out. Because the more you know yourself, the less you'll need to rely upon the approval of others.

And the next time someone lets you down ... breaks your heart ... or walks out on you, remember this rule: Don't cry. Don't shed a single tear for a person who doesn't believe in you. And don't look for their replacement, either. Don't look for someone to wipe away your tears. Instead of wiping away your tears, wipe away the people who made you cry.

Do Something Better

Are you as good as you can be or can you still get better? Yeah. Me too.

The only way things get better for you is when you get better. Good advice there.

We all want to get better, but how do we do it? How do we get better?

Lots of people get confused because they try to do too much at once. Then they get caught in overwhelm mode and that's how they get stuck.

That's why baby steps are much more useful in the long run … and even in the short run. Step by step. And today can be your first one.

A little bit at a time. Not all at once. A little bit today, a little bit tomorrow, and a little bit the next day.

So welcome to today. A brand new chance to change and get better. Use it wisely.

And don't get impatient with yourself while you're learning this new process. You're still being baked. Your cake is still soft in the middle. Don't keep checking on it. Don't keep poking it to see if it's finished yet.

You're gonna be a beautiful cake someday.

Say Something Better

Wanna try something that will change your life? Whenever you're about to find fault with someone, ask yourself this question, "What fault of my own most closely resembles the one I am about to criticize?"

Kindness is lending someone your strength instead of reminding them of their weakness. Let's take it even further. Try this for a goal:

Speak to people in such a way that they will love to listen to you. Listen to people in such a way that they will love to speak to you. Be somebody who makes everybody feel like a somebody.

How do we do that? By avoiding negative talk and becoming an encourager. This world has enough critics already. We don't need any more critics. We have more than enough of those.

But uplifters, elevators, and encouragers are always needed. Let's fill those roles in life. Because throughout every generation, those are the people who have always been in short supply.

Yesterday

Sometimes we don't give ourselves enough credit. Sometimes we don't believe in ourselves as much as we believe in other people. We've learned to think that way. But don't believe everything you think. Start thinking about what you've been thinking about.

Because while you're busy doubting yourself, other people are intimidated by your potential. Instead of doubting yourself, learn to doubt your doubts.

And don't beat up on yourself about your past. Forget about yesterday. Who you were yesterday is not necessarily an accurate prediction of who you are capable of becoming tomorrow. So get a ladder and get over it.

Get over yourself too. Get past your past. It's ancient history. There's no future in history. Stop letting who you were talk you out of who you're becoming. Stop looking in the rear view mirror. Stop looking behind you at your past. Don't bring your past into your future. Because when you examine the past closely, you'll find that nostalgia … isn't quite what it used to be.

And—always remember—yesterday ended last night.

I Can. I Shall. I Must. I Do. And I Am.

Did someone ever tell you that you can't do something? Yeah, me too. It's happened to me a million times. It's happened to lots of high achievers throughout history. Most great accomplishments were declared impossible right before they were done.

That discouraging voice of doom sounds just like this: "You can't."

I've heard those two horrible words a lot. I used to hear them so much I couldn't stand it. But I don't hear those words anymore. Know why? I've trained myself to tune out those discouraging voices.

I don't listen to those voices from other people. Those voices don't tell me what's possible for me. They tell me what's possible for them. I don't listen to those voices from other people any longer. More importantly, I don't listen to those voices from myself.

So the next time someone tells me, "You can't," know what I tell them? "I can. I shall. I must. I do. And I am."

You just sit there on the sidelines and watch. And please excuse me while I tune you out. Because a person who declares something is impossible … should never interrupt a person who's in the process of doing it.

Job or Career?

I think I'm having a mid-life existential crisis. Is it possible to do that at twenty-five? Maybe I'm just a fast learner and I'm ahead of schedule.

I'm growing increasingly dissatisfied with my job. I thought I wanted a career. Turns out I just wanted a regular paycheck each week. Somehow I thought it would all be a little more rewarding than it's turned out to be.

I always visualized myself in the same line of work I'm in now. I set my sights on this job back when I was in middle school. Seemed like a great industry and a perfect fit for my unique set of skills, talents, and aptitudes.

However … working at my dream job has taught me that we never really grow up. We only learn how to act in public.

A bus station is where a bus stops. A train station is where a train stops. At my place of employment, I have a work station. That gives you an idea of how much work I actually get done around there. Didn't start out that way, but I've picked up some bad habits being around my coworkers over the past two or three years.

They all seemed so bright then I first started. All of my coworkers. But looks can be deceiving. Remember, light travels much faster than sound. That's why some people look bright until you hear them speak. Pretty clever, right? But what's really clever is finding a way to avoid going down that same underperforming road myself. I'm putting that in my calendar. Writing that on my list of things to do for today. And maybe even tomorrow.

Walk into any Bookstore

Walk into any bookstore. You'll find rows and rows of books on success. Rows and rows of books on diet and nutrition. Therefore, we should all be rich, healthy, fit, and successful, right? We should all be millionaires with six-packs.

There's no shortage of information. There's a shortage of effort and motivation.

Do you see where I'm going? Do you ever feel like we've lost something in our generation? I very rarely meet anyone today with any kind of work ethic. I see this at my job every day. Before I got out into the real world, I saw it in school every day.

What happened to going the extra mile? People go to work for eight hours, and maybe turn in two hours of actual, genuine productivity. People go to work and step into this weird "gray zone." They're never fully present at their jobs. After work, they're never fully present at home, either.

Not here nor there. Neither fish nor fowl. Distracted, disassociated, dis-involved. Pretty much dis-everything.

Don't let that be you. Find what it is that sets your soul on fire and go after it. Doesn't have to be money and finances. It doesn't have to be health and fitness. It can be whatever you want, whatever speaks to you.

Because you can be a millionaire with a six-pack in any area of your life. The best part is … you get to choose. You always get to decide what to focus your attention on.

The Fear Door

Everything you've ever wanted is on the other side of fear. On the other side of that big, nasty Fear Door …

Yes. The Fear Door.

Well, let me tell you something about that door, my beautiful brothers and sisters. That's the door that leads us right out of our comfort zones. But that's also the door that—when locked and bolted—stops so many people from moving forward in life.

All the gifts and blessings of this world are on the other side of that fear door. So do whatever you've gotta do to walk yourself straight through that doorway. Open the door if you can. Bring in a wrecking ball and break down that door if you must. Whatever you have to do, do it. If you need to take a different approach, then take a different approach. Maybe you have to be a little sneaky to get the job done. Maybe you have to take the hinges off that door and slide yourself right through when nobody's watching.

Whatever your approach, make sure you remember what's waiting for you on the other side of That Fear Door. Freedom is there. Freedom from fear. Freedom from whatever's holding you back. Freedom to claim every good thing you've ever wanted for yourself and your loved ones. Every good thing in life is waiting for you … on the other side of fear. On the other side of That Fear Door.

Make your decision today to step through that door and claim it. Don't be afraid. Make fear … fear you.

Try Something Different

Yesterday started out kinda rough. I almost lost my temper, and I don't do that too much anymore. I'll be honest with you. You know what set me off? My computer. My computer beat me at chess. I had a hard time accepting that loss ... I guess it turned into an ego thing. Because I'm pretty good at chess. So I decided to go for two out of three. Wouldn't you know it? I tried again and that computer beat me again. Beat me two straight.

Well, I started thinking. This computer might beat me at chess, but it's no match for me at kickboxing. I got up from my chair. Put up my hands ... and prepared to unload. Fortunately, I stopped myself before I threw that kick. Before I proved that supposition about my superiority over my beautiful, highly intelligent machine in kickboxing.

And that's my takeaway and my lesson from almost losing my temper yesterday.

Don't get too attached to your first idea ... or your first way of doing things. Don't get too attached to your mistakes. Don't cling to a mistake. Don't keep going back to mistakes you been making just because you've spent a lot of time making them. You're not stuck with the way you are. Get up, dust yourself off, and try again. Try something new.

Try something different. You might get a better result. There's always a chance you'll stumble onto something better if you learn to step back, take a breath, calm yourself down, and try something new.

Trying To Fit In

You are special. You were made to stand out. So answer this question. Why are you always trying to fit in?

Anybody who ever accomplished anything exceptional, extraordinary, anything worth emulating ... was a loner and an outcast. Ridiculed by everyone around them ... especially those closest to them.

And yet, people spend their whole lives trying to fit in. People are afraid to be who they really are.

Why? When you become the person you're supposed to be, you become unstoppable. You become one of those rare people who fulfills their destiny ... and inspires other people to fulfill their destinies too.

So if you really want to fit in with someone ... why not those type of people? The best of the best. The high achievers. The great thinkers. The Wright Brothers, Amelia Earhardt, Thomas Edison, Steve Jobs, Elon Musk.

How about Winston Churchill, Ghandi, Martin Luther King, Nelson Mandela, Mother Teresa, Mary Shelley, Madame Curie, Marcus Aurelius, Joan of Arc, the Founding Fathers.

How about Lincoln? How does Abraham Lincoln grab you?

Wanna fit in with the crowd? Great. Then find the best crowd that ever existed in all of human history. Fit in with those guys. Emulate someone from that crowd. Find your inner Lincoln.

Money and Happiness

If necessity is the mother of invention, then why is so much unnecessary stuff invented? Economics, that's why. People trying to make money. Capitalism. Crass commercialism. Trying to invent new and innovative products ... and find new and innovative ways to separate people from their money.

Is that unethical? I don't know. In a perfect world, everybody would do the right thing. Everybody would have enough money to pay their bills. Enough food to eat. Everybody would be nice to each other.

That would be nice. Nice would be nice. Nice is always nice.

Unfortunately, we don't live in a perfect world. We live in a highly imperfect world. Perhaps you've noticed that. But human beings are highly imperfect too. ... so maybe we're a perfect match for this highly imperfect world we were all flung into at birth.

And in my humble opinion, money is an imperfect tool to help us all find happiness. Money can't buy happiness. Money just helps people look for happiness in more shiny, new places than they could before.

So don't chase money for your happiness. Find your happiness first. Then ... make the money chase you.

Mike Kimmel

Random Acts of Coffee

Are you a coffee-holic like me? Well then, maybe you can relate.

One day, I was in line for coffee at my very favorite place. You know the one I mean. It's probably your very favorite place too. I wasn't in the store this time, but I was going through the drive-through. This was when we were experiencing all that craziness.

Do you remember when we were in the middle of all that crazy quarantine? I think we're all gonna remember those days for a long, long time. Maybe you can relate.

I was having kind of a bad day. Wearing my mask and gloves. Feeling pretty stuffed up ... and grumpy too.

Then I get up to the front of the line ... order my coffee like I always do. I pick up my coffee ... and the pretty young girl with the nose ring tells me it's free. The car in front of me already paid. Because the car in front of him had paid for him! And that had been happening all day. One customer started it ... and everyone else started paying it forward.

Because even though everyone was feeling down and grumpy, we all made the same decision that glorious day: To treat the world better than the world was treating us. Doesn't matter how you feel. What matters is what you do. And you can bless someone with an act of kindness any time ... even when you don't particularly feel like doing it.

The Great Protector

Lately, I feel like I have a second job. I'm The Great Protector. I have to protect people from something very dangerous. I have to protect people from themselves.

Because people are walking around, driving around completely distracted. In a fog. In a stupor. Not even looking at the environment in front of them. Guess what they are looking at? Correct.

That blinking, beeping, flashing, pulsating shiny object in their hands. Looking down at their phones. Of course, of course. Like a pack of hypnotized automatons. Like a bunch of zombies. Like a pack of lemmings about to run themselves off a cliff.

And guess what's the only thing standing between them and oblivion? Correct again. Yours truly, The Great Protector. I'm extra cautious driving ... and even walking or jogging through the neighborhood. Trying to help distracted people avoid a crash or a fall.

I don't even think it's their fault. Maybe it's the way they've been conditioned in the last few years. Conditioned by their environment and the entire distracted culture. Please understand that I'm not blaming them and I'm not passing judgement. I'm just acknowledging an uncomfortable fact. And an equally uncomfortable responsibility I've recently acquired to help deal with that fact ... and help alleviate the growing danger people pose to themselves.

I didn't ask for this new job. It was thrust upon me. And that's okay. Responsibility is responsibility. Doesn't matter whether you choose it ... or it chooses you. We still have to step up and claim it.

Mike Kimmel

The Flat Earther

People used to laugh at my grandpa. Not to his face, but behind his back, for sure. They called him a Flat Earther. Meaning he was living in the past, not up on current thinking, ideas, and beliefs. Maybe even a conspiracy nut too.

Grandpa kept a big pile of money at home. I saw it once. It must have been in the thousands. Behind the dresser in his bedroom … in a little metal strongbox, Grandpa kept a great big wad of cold, hard cash.

My grandfather had been through some rough times. Rougher than rough, actually. Guess he'd seen a few things in his life. Lost his whole family. Served in the army. Captured. Prisoner of war. Lived through the Great Depression.

How can you not be nervous after you've experienced things like that? So I give my grandfather credit for trying as hard as he does. Because he does try hard to be optimistic. He tries to look for the best in the world. But it's hard for him.

Somedays all he can do is a little bit. But for a lot of people out there, a little, tiny sliver of hope is all they've got. So don't laugh behind their backs. Try to help them. Because it's not easy trying to keep a little, tiny sliver of hope alive.

The Big Lie

Somebody told me the big lie today. I've been hearing it a lot lately, so I guess I'm getting pretty good at recognizing that big old nasty fabrication whenever I hear it slither out of someone's mouth these days.

Give up? Wanna know what it is?

Fine. That's the lie. Yeah, I'm fine. The Fine Lie. I asked a co-worker at my job how he's doing and he said, "Fine. I'm fine."

Didn't look fine. Hair was a mess, fingernails all bitten down to the nubs, and the guy must have put on twenty pounds in the last month. I don't wanna sound rude, but he smelled a little funky too.

That's not fine. Nothing about that is fine.

But maybe we gotta dig a little deeper. Ask better questions. More probing questions … but without pushing anybody too hard.

A better question nowadays is, "Are you okay?" Think about it. "Are you okay?" shows someone you're interested and you care. It tells someone in trouble that you have a sympathetic ear. That you're a potential sounding board … in case they're really not okay. And maybe you can help.

"Are you okay" will always open a door for deeper conversations in life. So that's my new question. And I find it's a pretty good lie detector too. So don't let someone tell you they're fine … when you can plainly see that they're hanging on by a thread.

Mike Kimmel

Twenty Minutes

What can you do with twenty minutes? Doesn't sound like a lot of time, and on the surface, it's really not. Just a twenty-minute sliver of time. But time is relative, as they say.

Time is precious. I like to be productive with my time. That's when I'm happiest.

Unfortunately, that's not always possible because some people will waste your time.

Like my friend Cody.

Cody is consistently twenty minutes late. That's hard-wired into Cody's DNA, and not you, me, or any other known or unknown force on the face of this planet is gonna change that for my dear, close, personal friend Cody.

So I've learned to adapt. I've found a way to be productive ... with even a twenty-minute sliver of time. That might normally go to waste. Here's how. I wait twenty minutes ... like a good friend to Cody. And I use that time productively ... like a good friend to myself.

I'll always have a class assignment with me to work on. I'll always have emails I can catch up on. I'll always have my sketchbook so I can draw.

So you see, whenever I meet Cody, I factor twenty extra minutes of productivity into my day. And I can't say I came to this realization quickly. Because wisdom is more of a slow cooker than a microwave. But wisdom so often never arrives ... so we shouldn't beat up on ourselves too much when it shows up a little late. Even twenty minutes.

Wait Thirty Minutes

It rained all morning. But I had to go out to the library to pick up a book. It's only a few blocks from my house. I didn't even need to drive.

So I decided to go to that library and I got myself soaked through and through. Soaked down to the skin. Soaked and stressed.

Then I noticed something. Right after I got home ... and got out of my soaking wet clothes ... and opened up my soaking wet book, the sun came out. If I had waited thirty minutes, I could have avoided all that mess and stress.

Many storms in life will pass if you wait a little while ... and give them time to dissipate and scatter.

Okay, maybe some storms take longer than thirty minutes to pass. I get that. I do. Totally get it.

But thirty minutes is a pretty good start. There's plenty of storms, plenty of problems in life that will begin to dissipate, scatter, disappear ... and never bother you again.

If you start to develop a little more patience ... and wait thirty minutes ... to give them time to excuse themselves ... and walk right on out of your life.

Mike Kimmel

Bird Watching

Some college friends invited me to go bird watching. Right, bird watching. Ornithology, they call it. Some of them took classes in the subject when we were in school. I've been out of college for "x" number of years, but I like to stay in touch with my old friends. They're good people.

But ... bird watching? Really? To me, that's about as exciting as cutting an apple in half and watching it turn brown. No thanks. I grew up in the city. The big, bad city. I know sparrows and pigeons. Those are the only birds I'm acquainted with. Add squirrels to the mix, and that's the limit of my personal wildlife adventures and interactions. They're my only points of contact.

My old college friends pointed out all the varieties of birds. They explained the differences between them. They took notes and drew pictures in their little bird watching notebooks. They even bought me a little bird watching notebook too. That was a sweet little gift.

This was a whole new world I'd never experienced. Honestly, I never noticed all those different birds. But you know what I did notice? The whole time I was out there bird-watching with my old college friends ... I never once looked at my phone.

Here's my observation. I'm not sure if bird watching is exactly right for me ... but I think everyone should do something every day ... that makes us forget to check our phones.

The People Watcher

Can I tell you a secret?

I watch. I'm a people watcher. An observer of humanity. And there's a heck of a lot to observe, I'll tell you that right now. Sometimes good... sometimes bad... sometimes indifferent. But all definitely ... observable. Worthy of being watched. For one reason or another.

I don't even feel the urge to participate ... most of the time. I'm usually happy just watching. Does that sound weird to you? Yeah ... I guess it does to me too.

Sometimes I think I came from another planet. And other times ... well ... I'm sure of it. And if I really am from another planet, then the frailties of human existence need not apply to me. Because I don't have those issues. Greed. Anger. Pettiness. Impatience. Unforgiveness. Intolerance. Gossip. Mean-spiritedness. One-upmanship. None of that for me.

So I repeat. Does this sound weird? Maybe.

But I think we each have to embrace our own inner weirdo. You're not me, and I'm not you. We can't be each other. But we can be the best versions of ourselves. That's what we have to do. Instead of becoming good imitations of what someone else wants us to be. Oscar Wilde said, "Be yourself. Everyone else is already taken." Good advice.

And if you don't believe me ... or him ... then spend a little time in solitude ... just observing humanity. Don't talk. Just watch. You'll see.

Mike Kimmel

The DNA Test

I did that little DNA test thingy that everyone keeps talking about. You know the one, right? I knew I had some British in me, but now I found out I'm related to Jack the Ripper.

Jack the Ripper?!

You gotta be kidding me! If I have to be related to someone famous from England, why couldn't it be someone good? Why couldn't I be related to the Beatles?! What would be the harm in that? Maybe I could have inherited some of that musical talent they had. And some of their songwriting skill. Not to mention my fair share of all those royalties when they sing "Yesterday."

But no!! My yesterday doesn't have any percentage of the Beatles in it. Not even Ringo, the little one. My yesterday goes way back to the 1800s. And what kind of royalties am I gonna get from being related to Jack the Ripper?! Ten percent off all sharpening services for my big, giant serial killer knife?

Doesn't do me any good because I don't have a big, giant serial killer knife like Jack the Ripper used. And If I did, I'd use it for cooking, not killing.

But I do have a guitar like the Beatles used. And I can use it to make beautiful music just like they did. Whether I'm related to them or not. So I guess what I'm saying is ... it doesn't matter who I'm descended from ... or not descended from.

What's really important is the imprint I leave on history with my own unique set of gifts and talents. What's important is my own DNA.

I Bought a Vintage Car

I bought a vintage car. It's the same age as me. Isn't that something? It was built the same year I was born. Came off the assembly line the same time I did.

The chassis is a little beat up. Kinda like my own. They're in just about the same kinda shape. We've both taken some major hits. We've both been driven down some rough roads. Rougher than rough. As a matter of fact, some of those roads weren't even paved. And I can promise you that I felt every bump along the way.

But I've got plans for this vintage car. I'm gonna rebuild her. Tear her apart so I can build her back up to where she needs to be.

And not just the cosmetic stuff, either. I'm gonna dig down deep inside … and do all that hard internal work people never see … to keep this vintage machine in perfect working condition year after year after year.

And I know it's not gonna be easy. Gonna have to get down and dirty. And be prepared to roll up my sleeves and stay committed for the long haul.

In the process, I'm gonna do some deep, reconstructive, internal work on myself. And maybe I can build myself back up to where I need to be too.

Mike Kimmel

How Do We Decide?

Do you eat a lot of protein? It's a simple question. It's none of my business, but there is a reason I'm asking. I played sports most of my life. Team sports. Individual sports. Pretty much everything. And most of the other athletes I knew ate a ton of protein. They ate protein every day. That seems to be the norm, I guess.

Beef, chicken, fish, pork. Some of them even eat venison. Deer meat. To each his own. Or her own, because all the female athletes I knew were hard-core carnivores too.

That's all fine. My question, though, is how do we decide? No, no, no, not decide between beef and chicken and fish and pork ... and venison ... but between all those delectable standard choices ... and all of the *non-standard* choices, as well.

The "other" animals. The ones we don't eat. The ones we keep as pets ... or the ones we bring our children to see at the petting zoo. For example, some people eat rabbit, but my little daughter has a pet rabbit, so I just couldn't. It's super cute.

Should that be our measuring stick, though? Do we decide whether to eat it or play with it based upon how cute it is ... or how cute it isn't? That doesn't seem right either. How about squirrel? I know, I know, but they eat squirrel meat in a lot of places around the world. Elvis Presley ate squirrel. I'm not judging. Far be it from me to criticize Elvis. He loved squirrel.

And that explains a lot. Because, to tell you the truth, I never could wrap my brain around those blue suede shoes.

First, Last, and Only

Okay, I should explain. I have a personality quirk. Make that several personality quirks, but the one I want to talk about deals with restaurants. If I walk into a restaurant and I don't feel welcome ... and that my patronage of that particular establishment is valued ... well, then, guess what? I'm out of there. I will not stay. Good night and good luck. Exit, stage left, brothers and sisters.

Maybe this sounds harsh, but here are my deal breakers.

One. They kept us waiting too long before seating us.

Two. I didn't like the table. Too small. Too dirty. Too wobbly. Too close to the kitchen. Too close to the bathroom.

Three. Speaking of that bathroom, if I need to use it ... and it looks and smells like a truck stop rest room on Route 66 ... well then, Sayonara, baby.

One strike, and you're out. If a restaurant commits any one of those violations on my watch, then I'm history. So long, Charlie.

The police may give you three strikes, but I only offer one. I'm a smaller operation, and can't afford second chances. They get one chance with me. If they've just used it up ... then that was my first, last, and only time inside their doors. They have lost me as a customer forever.

Mike Kimmel

Good Bad Role Models

When I was a kid I used to wish I had some good role models. But I didn't. The area I grew up in was a little rough, to tell you the truth. I didn't have any good role models, but I had a lot of bad role models. Bad role models were everywhere.

Seemed like there were millions of them. Drunks. Druggies. Drug Dealers. Liars. Cheaters. Bullies. Deadbeats. Scammers. Shoplifters. And other questionable types who were difficult to categorize from afar. Believe me, I never got close enough to scrutinize, analyze ... or categorize.

Instead, I said to myself, "Self, let me use what I have available. Let me use these bad role models. That could be helpful." I looked around and said, "I don't wanna be like him, I don't wanna be like her, and I definitely don't want to be like that guy." I did this daily ... and it worked.

So even though I couldn't find any good role models, I used the negative role models in the same way other kids ... from better neighborhoods ... used their positive role models.

I guess those bad examples turned out to be pretty good for me. Those people were really good at being really bad. They set the bar extraordinarily low. And I've done a decent job of avoiding turning out the way they did. Because they were really good at setting a really bad example. By demonstrating all the awful, horrible actions and qualities I never wanted to duplicate in my own life.

The Statute of Limitations

I had a rough childhood. As a matter of fact, it was rougher than rough. Dad made it that way. He was rough on my mom. Yeah, he was rough on me too. Mom and Dad split when I was pretty young. In middle school.

You would think things would get better after that, but they didn't. I don't think my mom was cut out to be a single mother. There was never enough money. Never enough time. Most of all, there was never enough peace.

But I'm not in middle school anymore. I've learned a few things. Let me tell you my philosophy of life. Here it is in a nutshell. Or a clamshell. Or wherever kinda shell you want to put it in.

The statute of limitations on parental crimes runs out when you're twenty-five.

After age twenty-five, you're responsible for your own life. Responsible for figuring it all out. For figuring yourself out. Nobody knows you better than you. And you're the one who's responsible for making yourself happy or miserable. Your choice. Both options are available given your unique set of circumstances.

There is no one right path. You make the path when you walk. So get up and get moving. Walk yourself into your future. And remember, your future is up to you, so make sure you walk yourself into the exact kind of future you want to create.

That's a future with no excuses. And no one to blame—or congratulate—except yourself. Nope. Not even your parents.

Mike Kimmel

Email Etiquette

Has anyone ever talked with you about email etiquette? It's a topic that's not often discussed, but I think it should be.

Yeah, yeah, I know. Most of the people our age probably text more than we email. I get it. I do. And I've been there too.

But there are times when it's not appropriate to text, right? Like job interviews, requesting college transcripts, writing to update your personal information with your bank or credit union. You're just not gonna text, tweet, or hashtag your way through any of those particular interactions.

And they are particular interactions. Meaning they are unique occurrences ... and require you to employ a unique method of communication.

Email. Which stands for electronic mail. Which you probably knew already. But what you probably didn't know is that people's email communication skills have become sloppy through inaction and misuse. This leads us to present ourselves in a less than favorable light when it's most important to present ourselves in a highly favorable light.

Solution. Turn up that favorable light. Put your thinking cap on. Think about what you're writing about before you start writing about what you're thinking about.

Example, don't use non-words like LOL, IMO, and IDK. Those are okay for texting. Not okay for email ... not okay for snail mail or longhand either.

It's okay. Breathe. You can do this. It's just a question of relearning a good old skill. And unlearning a bad new habit.

And ... the same way you learned to abbreviate everything? That's the same skill set you can use to become more creative, more specific, and more varied in your use of written language.

Class dismissed.

Mike Kimmel

About Fifty Percent

There's this older gentleman who lives in my neighborhood. Right down the block. He doesn't bother anybody, but he does something kinda strange.

I guess he's retired now and doesn't know what to do with himself. So he takes a chair—a beach chair—and carries it about half a block away. And he sits underneath this big shade tree in front of the library. There's a little branch library right down the street.

He just sits there all day. Sometimes he has a book. Sometimes he brings his tablet. He has his phone and he sits there making all his personal phone calls … too many personal phone calls … kinda embarrassing, actually. But I guess he doesn't know what to do with himself these days … and what to do with his free time.

I always wave when I walk by. And I have to walk by to get to my car. That's usually where I find parking. But this man doesn't always wave back. He waves back sometimes. About fifty percent of the time.

I don't know what to make of that. The short answer would be to get offended. To become so offended I stop waving and stop saying hello.

But that's not me. I try to be friendly with all my neighbors. But I don't want to be an idiot about it. And I don't want to bother somebody who wants to be left alone.

That's a conundrum. No easy answer. But I've decided I'm going to keep being me. I'm going to keep waving and saying hello. It doesn't matter if he answers me back ... or doesn't answer me back. Because nobody needs a friendly greeting so much as a person who doesn't have one to give.

Mike Kimmel

Exercising in the Park

I went to the park today to eat my lunch. I had a rough day, to tell you the truth. Sometimes I go to the park to de-stress when things start getting a little crazy. Like today.

I just wanted to be by myself. Didn't want to talk to anybody. But I noticed something that surprised me. There were all these people in the park exercising. I kinda didn't expect that. Sure, I've seen people walking and jogging in the park before. But this was different. Much more involved. There were five or six people doing yoga together. One of them seemed to be the teacher and the others were all the yoga students. They all brought their yoga mats to the park and they were doing their breathing and stretching exercises outside in the fresh air and sunshine.

Then I saw some guys playing soccer. Not kids, but grown men. And they had some serious skills. And uniforms. They must be part of an adult semi-pro league or something.

There were also a couple of big beefy guys lifting weights. They had all their dumbbells and kettlebells out in the grass and were taking turns doing some crazy weight lifting movements. Really wild. And they were screaming to encourage each other ... which was not only inspiring, but actually pretty funny to watch.

It all got me thinking about how people utilize their resources. Every resource available to them. And this park is a great resource for all kinds of people. People playing sports. People at all different levels of fitness. People in their twenties and senior citizens.

What they have in common is a creative approach to using their neighborhood resource in their own unique way.

And ... on the other side of the park, there were people having a nice quiet lunch ... just like me. Sure, the park is a great place for all kinds of workouts, but if you just want a nice, quiet lunch, or even a picnic ... the park is great for that too. Your park is the great equalizer.

It's whatever you want it to be. It's a little like water. It fits whatever kind of container you want to pour it into. You get to choose. How about that? Every day, you get to choose.

More importantly, it's a good place to go for people like me ... who are having kind of a rough day. Whether you want to eat a quiet lunch, throw some noisy kettlebells around ... or just sit there in nature and sing with the birds. Whatever you want. Do what you feel. The park is a gentleman. The park never tells you what to do.

Mike Kimmel

The Squirrels' Revenge

I guarantee you've never heard this one before. I know this couple, Susie and Johnny. Really good friends of mine in Houston, Texas. Well … after they got married, they bought their first house. They were so excited. Beautiful house. Big backyard. Big, green trees. Beautiful.

Just one problem. They had an issue with field mice. Little critters running around the backyard. Making all kinds of mess. Ripping up the flower beds, chewing holes in stuff. Pretty much running rough-shod over that entire backyard territory.

So Susie and Johnny did what any self-respecting Texans would do. No, they didn't shoot 'em, but they set out those little plastic traps with poison for the mice to walk into. You know the ones I'm talking about, right?

And the mice did just that. That worked. Got rid of the mice. Thinned out that herd. But guess what? There were other little critters out there about the same size. They walked into those poison traps too. Cute little critters.

Baby squirrels.

The traps were too small for the Mama and Papa squirrels to squeeze themselves into, but the little, itty-bitty baby squirrels could just walk right in. Grab themselves a tasty little snack of poisoned mouse food. Yum. Yum.

Those baby squirrels went belly up. Susie and Johnny found their little dead squirrel bodies on the patio. Horrible. They felt terrible about it. But the Mama and Papa Squirrels felt even worse. And they showed it. They started waiting for my friends to come out back—and then they'd throw acorns at them! The big squirrels started waiting for my friends from up high in the trees. Started throwing acorns at them. Bouncing those acorns off Susie and Johnny's heads whenever they could. This went on for years ... until those squirrels either died of old age or moved away in disgust.

How weird is this? Weird enough to be true. Truth is stranger than fiction.

And there's a lesson to be learned here. Word to the wise for every new homeowner. Be careful what you spread around in your community. Spread love, not poison. You don't wanna make enemies with the locals. Not even four-legged locals. Apparently, they hold a grudge for life.

My Blind Date

I had a blind date last night. No, don't even say it, okay? I'm not asking for anyone's advice, opinion, or permission, thank you very much. It's my social calendar and I'll fill it up or leave it blank as I see fit.

I never liked blind dates. But ever since I split with Alex, I've been spending a little too much time alone ... and that's not good either. Hence, the blind date.

So people need to cut me a little slack. Two reasons. One, because I'm lonely. And two, because I can use the word "hence" properly in a sentence. So at least you know I'm educated and have good grammar. But good grammar doesn't make me less lonely.

Hence the blind date. Which is uncomfortable enough by itself, and certainly did not require a substandard restaurant choice to add to the pervasive discomfiture. Nevertheless, that's the place the two of us picked ... so now you have a pretty good snapshot of the way my evening went last night.

Let me give you the short version. Wrong restaurant on the wrong night with the wrong person. I think that pretty much covers it.

I figured something out last night just as my blind date was winding down ... uh, plummeting down to its unnatural conclusion. It's no fun sitting home by yourself on a Saturday night feeling lonely. But it sure beats being out with someone new ... and still feeling lonely. That's against the rules.

Actually makes me appreciate being by myself again. And I'm gonna keep working on myself by myself for myself. Because I know how to be pleasant and keep myself good company when I'm alone.

I've had enough practice lately, that's for sure.

Autonomy

When was the last time you achieved autonomy? When was the last time you achieved a complete sense of mastery and control over your life?

I'm not trying to pick on you today. I promise. I'm not trying to put you down, pull you down, or push you around. I'm just trying to point something out.

It's something we all need to shine a spotlight on from time to time. Bring it to the forefront of our own self-awareness. Yes. Self-awareness. We spend so much time, effort and energy trying to stay aware of what's happening out there in the external world that we sometimes forget to keep a discerning eye … on ourselves.

We need to keep an eye on ourselves … and remind ourselves daily that we are in charge of our own lives. We all need to vigorously guard our unique, individual autonomy. Yes, myself included. I don't get a pass just because I'm pointing this out … though I truly wish I did.

For most of us, sad to say, our autonomy is slipping away … if we ever really had a handle on it to begin with.

Sure, we've got choices … but someone-something-somewhere is controlling all the available options you have to choose from. It's a rigged game. The dice are loaded. And the powers that be figured out long before we were born … how to manipulate us. How to beat us before we even realize we're in a fight.

Don't be manipulated. Pull your own strings. That starts with self-awareness. Open your eyes and remind yourself daily that you are the only one who can think inside your mind. You are the one in charge of your own mind ... your own thought processes ... your own life ... and your own autonomy.

When the Smoke Clears

I found the perfect apartment. It's exactly the kind of place I've always visualized myself in. Great location, plenty of room, ground floor, with a little entrance off the courtyard. Know what's the best part of all? There's this sweet little backyard patio area that's completely private … and self-enclosed.

As soon as I saw that private little backyard … I said, "I'll take it!" I always wanted a little place like that where I could relax, be by myself, meditate, and de-compress. Where I can write, draw, and paint without anyone interrupting me for hours and hours … to my heart's content.

I couldn't wait to move in, set up my easel … and really start getting my portfolio together. Finally.

Then, my first day out in my little backyard … BAM … I smelled it! Cigarette smoke! No … can't be! Where the heck is it coming from? Ah … the apartment next door. Dang! Okay, I'll try later. Later that day … BAM … more cigarette smoke … from the building across the alley. Man, oh, man … I went back inside and thought I'd try again later. After the smoke clears.

That night, I tried again and learned my neighbors are on a strict schedule. At 6:00 PM, the cigarettes stop and the marijuana begins. You can't even make this stuff up. I wish I were making it up. But unfortunately it's become my new reality. But that's okay … because I've now learned to clear the smoke from my mind.

When I clear the smoke from my mind ... it doesn't matter what anybody else does or doesn't do. What they smoke or don't smoke. What matters is my focus. I've now become inner-directed, rather than outer-directed. I don't need a special little place outside with a meditation garden to be creative. I can do that by myself and for myself ... and with myself ... any time I want ... right inside my own creative, smoke-free, unclouded head.

Visiting Aunt Cathy

I went to visit my Aunt Cathy last weekend. I was sent, actually. Mom asked me to go stay with her for the weekend. A mercy mission, for sure.

Aunt Cathy is my mom's big sister. She's the oldest, but somehow … how do I say this nicely? Aunt Cathy just never seems to get it together. She's always in the middle of some kind of mess or dealing with some new, unexpected drama in her life. She's got more problems than a math book.

And it's a shame, because she's really a sweetheart. I absolutely adore her. But she's a total hot mess … a train wreck … and she's always been that way. Ever since she was a teenager, from what Mom tells me. She's in her fifties now.

I've been on these mercy missions before. It's been a while. Sometimes I forget how to handle her best. When I got there, the place was a mess. Junk and clothes thrown everywhere. Like she hadn't cleaned up in months.

I was a little startled. But I said, "Hey. What's up? How you doing?"

Big mistake. Never ask a woman eating ice cream directly from the container how she's doing. Aunt Cathy totally lost it. Started crying on my shoulder, telling me all the creepy details of her latest romantic disappointment, how her new job's not working out, how she never feels good anymore, how the neighbors keep her up all night, how she's ready to give up, how she's been feeling unworthy, et cetera, et cetera, et cetera.

I wish I had magic words to wash it away for her. I don't have any magic words. But sometimes, you don't need magic words. Just magic ears. I listened to my aunt all night. After a while, she started to feel better. Maybe that's what people need most when they're hurting ... just someone to listen—and without judging. That, I can handle. Ernest Hemingway said that when people talk, we should really listen ... and listen completely. Most people never listen. Hemingway was a smart man. He knew what he was talking about.

I know I don't have all the answers. But when I don't know what to do, I can always settle down and listen to Ernest Hemingway's wise advice. And I can always settle down and listen to my beautiful Aunt Cathy trying to work her life out too ... with no judgment.

Mike Kimmel

Anatomy of a Compliment

What's the best way to feel real good about yourself? Don't worry. It's not a trick question. The best way to feel good about yourself is to help someone else feel good about himself. Or herself ... as the case may be. Themselves.

That's what human beings are here for. That's why we came to this planet. And it's something we're good at. We may not realize we're good at it ... because we don't practice. But we should practice. Because the more we practice ... the better we'll get at this particular skill. And it's a skill well worth developing, I can promise you that.

Now ... making our fellow humans feel good about themselves sounds cool, right? Right? Of course right. But how? How do we do it? How do we put this worthy ideal into action?

I'm glad you asked that question.

By paying a sincere compliment, that's how. There's no better way to lift someone up than through the fine art of honest complimentation. That's not a real word, but it's definitely a real thing.

And the two best things to compliment are ... a person's accomplishments and a person's possessions. With accomplishments, you're recognizing something good they did ... like a job they got, a test they passed, or a talent they developed. Complimenting their possessions tells them they have good taste. You like the shoes they picked out ... the color they're wearing ... or maybe the fragrance they put on today.

But don't compliment someone for being good looking. Prettiest woman in the room already knows she's the prettiest woman in the room. The handsomest guy too. And some guys are worse than girls ... when it comes to checking themselves out in the mirror, I mean.

So what I'm saying is ... don't be Captain Obvious. Dig deeper. Get more creative with your compliments. Your compliments will help people feel good about themselves. And they'll help you feel good about yourself too. Even if *you're* the prettiest or handsomest person in the room.

Mike Kimmel

The Honor of Disrespect

What is going on in this world lately? Why are people so disrespectful nowadays? I mean everyone.

Even little kids. Talking back to their parents and teachers. No respect for authority. No respect for their elders. What is up with that?

I don't want to focus on the negative, but it seems like I've been coming up against a lot of disrespect lately. More than normal these last couple of weeks, for sure. People just not treating me right. Talking sarcastic. Making fun of me. Putting me down.

And I've got a pretty thick skin. I know there's going to be people that are a little hard to take. But lately it seems like they're going for the blue ribbon or something. The blue ribbon of obnoxiousness.

My dad says people are doing about as well as they can. If they could do better, they would do better. Maybe if someone's disrespecting me, it's because he has no respect for himself. You can't give away something you don't have. If you ask me for a piece of gum, and I don't have any gum in my pocket, then I can't provide you with a piece of gum. I can't give you something I don't have for myself. Same with respect, dignity, appreciation, any good thing in life.

If I don't have that quality myself, then I surely can't demonstrate that quality on your behalf. But there's good news. I believe ... it's *a tremendous honor* to be disrespected by under-performers, bottom-feeders ... and plain old everyday jerks. That proves ... none of those creep-a-zoids can relate to you. They don't look at you and see similarities. They don't consider you a kindred spirit.

And that's good news. Because in my humble opinion, there is no greater stamp of approval in this world ... than the disrespect of dishonorable, disreputable, disrespectful people.

Mike Kimmel

An Inconvenient Convenience

I need your advice. They say advice is what you ask for when you already know the answer but wish you didn't.

Nevertheless, here goes ... something. A group of us went out to this nice restaurant. Not expensive, but nice.

I drove. Maybe not such a great idea ... because the restaurant my friends picked had valet parking. I hate valet parking. Is that wrong?

I won't give my car to a valet. Guess I picked up that habit from my parental units. They don't valet either. Never. If they go to a place that has valet parking ... they'll either leave and go somewhere else ... or park a million miles away and walk back.

It's not the money, okay? Honestly, it's not. Well ... maybe a little. Why should we pay extra to park at their restaurant when we're already paying to eat at their restaurant? Doesn't make good economic sense. It's like a double whammy. And, besides the money, I don't like somebody else driving my car. They move the seat, change the mirror ... and sometimes ... they stink up the whole vehicle!

Yes. There, I said it! Stink up the whole vehicle! One time this valet guy had such a strong cologne, I was smelling it for three weeks after!

What the heck is the point of all that?! Theoretically ... hypothetically ... valet parking is supposed to be a convenience. Right? Not an inconvenience. But if I have to fumigate the car, change the seat and mirrors back the way I like them ... and pay money for the privilege of doing so ... well ... I don't consider that very convenient.

And that's why I will not under any circumstances ... heretofore known or unknown ... participate in that highly inconvenient ritual of valet parking. Call me cheap if you want. I don't care. Here endeth the lesson.

Mike Kimmel

On the Backs of Envelopes

I write. Essays, poems, short stories, long stories. Fiction, non-fiction. Little bit of everything.

Maybe even a novel someday. Got a funny feeling ... one of those is in me too ... just screaming to come flying out. Because once I put pencil down to paper ... boom, that's it. It just starts flowing. Well, ninety-nine per cent of the time, anyway.

So my aunt and uncle bought me this beautiful leather journal to write in. Super nice. Looks super expensive too. Very thoughtful gift. Perfect book for me to write down all my ... short stories, long stories, fiction, non-fiction ... and maybe even that novel that's floating around inside my head.

Yes, indeed. It's the perfect book.

A little too perfect. That's the problem. Every time I put pencil down to paper ... I get all tensed up. Worried I'm gonna make a mistake. Which is really no big deal. But I worry I'm gonna write something imperfect in this perfect book ... and then have to scratch it all out.

And who wants to make a mistake in a beautiful leather writing journal that looks like it should be in a museum somewhere? That's why it's still blank. Just as blank as the day I received it.

And it will probably always stay blank. Because I get so nervous about messing up that perfect writing book ... that I do all my writing on scrap paper, post-it notes, and ... the backs of envelopes. That's right. I actually do my best writing on the backs of envelopes. I never worry about messing those up because they're already a mess. That really seems to free up my creativity.

So ... lately I've been writing some real good stuff. Real good. I guess that beautiful leather writing journal my aunt and uncle bought me has helped me a lot. It's helped me write my best stuff lately ... by not writing in it.

Mike Kimmel

Fifty-Two Bad Ones

I wrote something down. I don't know if it's any good or not, but I liked it. It was just an idea, but I let it simmer. In a day or two I turned it into a funny little story. No biggie. The whole thing was just a page or two.

But it felt good. The whole process. I liked the completion of it. Having the idea, writing it down, thinking about where it could go, and then turning it into a little, self-contained story. Something that could stand on its own with a beginning, middle, and end.

And now that it's done I can do something with it. If I want to. I can enter it in a contest, submit it to a newspaper or magazine, or just send it to my college alumni newsletter.

If I want to.

The point is … when it was just an idea percolating around inside my head … I couldn't do anything with it. I couldn't do anything with it because it wasn't tangible. It didn't exist on paper. It was a nice enough idea, but ideas are just little electrical impulses bopping around from one synapse in your brain to another.

And if you don't do something with those "nice enough" ideas, nobody knows you even have them. They don't exist anywhere outside your head. But this one does exist. I can print it out and touch it. If it's good, I can frame it. Hang it on the wall. If it's bad, I can tear it up. Toss it.

And you know what else I can do? I can do it all over again. I can repeat the entire process again and again. Wash, rinse, repeat. I can do that every week if I want to. By the end of the year, I'll have fifty-two individual little stories with a beginning, middle, and end. That's probably enough for my very first book.

Okay, okay, I know ... some of the stories are gonna be better than others. But you know what? I got a feeling if I can keep writing my little stories each and every week ... they'll keep getting better ... and it will be almost impossible to write fifty-two bad ones.

Pie in the Sky

When I got to college, everybody started asking me what I wanted to study. What I wanted to do with my life. I knew exactly what I wanted. I've known ever since I was a little kid.

I told family and friends I wanted to be an artist, a painter. Like Leonardo da Vinci, Michelangelo, Rembrandt, Goya, Picasso. And my hero, Vincent Van Gogh.

I'd like to paint big, beautiful canvases. I'd like to create my own solo shows of my original artwork in art galleries. Maybe even see my paintings hanging on the walls in a museum someday. Why not? We need to think big. Other artists' work hangs in museums. So why not mine? Think big. I thought my family would be proud. I thought they'd be supportive.

Unfortunately, it was just the opposite.

In fact, someone close to me really tried to shoot me down. Like they were trying to rain on my parade. This person called my dream ... are you ready? They called my artistic dreams ... "Pie in the Sky." Have you ever heard that? It's an old figure of speech.

This person meant that my dream was a fantasy, something floating around in the air. A will-o'-the-wisp.

But that's not even what "Pie in the Sky" means. Do you know what it actually refers to? Don't worry, most people don't. "Pie in the Sky" is a term used by long-distance truck drivers. It's a strategy to keep them going on their long hauls ... visualizing their favorite pie at their favorite truck stop on that route. Then, once they reach that destination, that "Pie in the Sky" becomes a reality on their plate! After that, it becomes a delicious memory. That's a whole lot more than a will-o'-the-wisp.

Vincent Van Gogh only sold one painting in his entire life. He earned the equivalent of thirty U.S. dollars during his lifetime from his artwork. But he's still inspiring people hundreds of years later. Yeah, I know. We've all got to make money. I get it. But I don't want to do work that just pays the bills.

I want to do work that sets my soul on fire.

Mike Kimmel

He Begged Me Not To Go

My father begged me not to go. He didn't ask. He begged. He knew I was making a mistake, but I had just turned eighteen. I was old enough to make my own decisions. Old enough to make my own mistakes.

That was the biggest argument I ever had with my father. I was young, strong, and full of confidence. The best athlete in my school. I was in fantastic shape back in those days. Worked out like crazy. I knew boot camp would be no big deal. I could walk right through those six weeks without breaking a sweat. I could walk right through my two years of military service. Like a big, fat nothing burger.

My father begged me not to go. He was in the service when he was my age. Sure, I knew it wasn't easy for him. He told me his stories. But he wasn't in the kind of physical condition I was in. He knew that. He knew I could handle myself too. Still … he begged me not to go.

Looking back, I don't know how I could have been so confident and so stupid at the same time. That takes some kind of talent, I'll tell you. And now, here I stand before you. Looking okay on the outside. Not like when I was eighteen, but still pretty good.

The outside's good. But the inside still needs some work. I don't sleep so well anymore. I saw things overseas I'll never forget. So horrible I can't talk about them. But I have to talk about them. My therapist says it's important to get it out so it's not all bottled up inside. I see the therapist twice a week now. It was three times before, but they cut me back to two. That's good. That's progress. They'll help me get a job soon too. Just part-time, but that's progress. That's a beginning.

Therapy helps a lot. My father drives me to my sessions and waits outside. The doctors don't want me to drive until I'm all better ... and my father doesn't want me taking the bus because of the high school kids and all their stupid jokes. Kids from the same school where I earned all those varsity letters and trophies and awards five hundred lifetimes ago.

Dad drives me twice a week. Sometimes we stop for a hot lunch on the way home. Sometimes it's barbecue, sometimes it's spaghetti and meatballs, and sometimes we share a pizza. I get along great with my father now. We never argue like we used to. We talk about everything. We have great conversations. I found out he's a very smart man.

He begged me not to go.

Mike Kimmel

The Rocky Marciano Technique

I'm good with my hands. I box. I'm not going to the Olympics any time soon, but I box. Grandpa taught me. He was a good fighter back in the day. Good enough to spar with a legend, Rocky Marciano … an absolutely devastating puncher.

Marciano was the only undefeated heavyweight champion. Nobody else … before or after … retired undefeated. Not Jack Dempsey. Not Joe Louis. Not Mike Tyson. Not even Muhammad Ali.

Unfortunately, he was a smaller guy, 190 pounds, with the shortest reach of any heavyweight champ. That's a tremendous disadvantage. That punching power was irrelevant if he couldn't reach his target.

To win, Marciano knew he'd have to learn to make the most of what nature gave him to work with.

And work with it he did. Rocky loved to exercise. Trained so long and so hard that his coaches had to turn out the lights in the gym to make him go home.

The way he trained was unusual too. He could spend three months in training camp before a big fight. He wouldn't change his diet, meet new people, take phone calls, or even open his mail before a big fight—for fear that something unexpected would distract him and get him slightly off his game.

He used a specially made heavy bag to develop the awesome punching power that sent so many opponents to dreamland. A heavy bag from a sporting goods store weighs 70 pounds. Rocky's bag weighed 300 pounds. Once he got that gigantic heavy bag swinging back and forth, he would crouch down so low, he could bob and weave underneath it as it moved. Marciano would get so low in the crouch that he could touch his toes.

His style was awkward, clumsy, unorthodox … and extremely effective. Because of his short reach, opponents could keep away. He couldn't get to their head or torso. So he hit their arms as they were covering up. Not super hard, but super consistent. Tap, tap, tap. By the twelfth or thirteenth round, an opponent's aching arms would drop … and the champ could land one of his deadly haymakers.

Rocky Marciano made the most of what he had—and developed a unique style that capitalized on his shortcomings. That style was so efficient that challengers with better technique and more polished skills could never defend against it.

Make up your mind … to make the most of what nature gave you too. Turn your own negatives into unstoppable positives. And develop patience like Rocky Marciano had. Tap, tap, tap at all your problems in life until they fall away, lie flat on their back … and can never hope to challenge you again.

Maybe all of us can learn to do that. And maybe fifty years from now, they'll be talking about us like we're talking about him.

Mike Kimmel

An Older Driver

I was ten minutes late to my job today. No big deal. I didn't get in trouble or anything. It was actually my first time ever being late.

It's not like me to be late. I'm not making excuses, but it wasn't really my fault. I got stuck behind another car driving very slow on the road I take. It's only one lane in each direction, so if you've got a slow-poke driver out there in front of you … well then … you become a slow-poke driver by default.

A couple of cars behind me were getting all agitated. Honking their horns and making hand gestures I didn't appreciate. You know how that goes. Definitely impatient. I don't know … it seems like people out on the road are a little more impatient than they were when I first started driving. And that was only a few years ago.

Maybe I'm missing something, but I've just never been a very impatient person. I guess I just don't see the benefit. I don't see the benefit to me or to anybody else. And I could tell the line of cars behind me did not agree.

But in this case, they were wrong and I was right. I was close enough to see that the driver in front of me was an elderly man. An older driver.

I have a lot of patience anyway, but I try to show a little extra patience when I see an older driver. Maybe because their reflexes are slower, and they forget things, and they've got a lot of aches and pains. And maybe because I'm going to be an older driver myself someday too. And I hope people will have patience with me.

Afterword

Feel free to adapt these monologues as you see fit for your own performances. If it helps you to change a name, location, or other detail within the text to make it better suited to your particular background, point of view, age, physical type, or skill set ... then please feel free to do so.

We're all wildly different, and a minor tweak in the script will sometimes make a major difference in helping us breathe life into the characters on the page. As long as you stay true to the overall intention of the pieces, these monologues should still work well for you.

The big picture goal in writing all the monologues has been to keep the individual storylines logical and user-friendly in pacing and character development. With this in mind, you may discover that these monologues—even the longer ones—will be relatively easy to memorize.

"The key to the future of the world is finding the optimistic stories and letting them be known."

~ Pete Seeger

Help Spread The Word

If you've enjoyed this book—and feel that it will benefit other actors, teachers, and coaches—please consider posting a short book review on your favorite social media platform or book-related website. Book reviews are very important for authors and help spread the word about their work to a broader audience, while increasing readership and visibility across multiple platforms.

Additionally, please consider recommending this book to your local public library or school. Schools and libraries can often purchase books at a significant discount. This will assist in making this material available to actors who may not be able to purchase copies for themselves.

If you need a little motivational boost, let's connect on social media for positive messages and updates. You'll find me on:

Facebook: **Mike Kimmel's Scenes for Teens**

Instagram: **@MikeKimmelAuthor**

Twitter: **@MikeKimmelActor**

Pinterest: **Mike Kimmel Actor-Author**

You can also visit my website **MikeKimmelAuthor.com** to read my free monthly blog. You'll find articles on acting, auditioning, and the entertainment industry, along with information on the other books in this series.

"The self is not something ready-made,
but something in continuous formation
through choice of action."

~ John Dewey

Recommended Reading

Acting for Films and TV by Leslie Abbott

Acting in Film by Michael Caine

Acting in Television Commercials for Fun and Profit by Squire Fridell

Adventures in the Screen Trade by William Goldman

An Actor Prepares by Constantin Stanislavski

An Agent Tells All by Tony Martinez

Audition by Michael Shurtleff

The Backstage Actor's Handbook by Sherry Eaker

Being an Actor by Simon Callow

A Book by Desi Arnaz

The Courage to Create by Rollo May

The Definitive Book of Body Language by Allan and Barbara Pease

Do One Thing Every Day That Scares You by Robie Rogge

The Dramatic Writer's Companion by Will Dunne

Ego is the Enemy by Ryan Holliday

Four Screenplays by Syd Field

Free Play: Improvisation in Life and Art by Stephen Nachmanovitch

Mike Kimmel

The Great Movies by Roger Ebert

Hollywood by Charles Bukowski

Hollywood Babylon by Kenneth Anger

How I Made a Hundred Movies in Hollywood and Never Lost a Dime by Roger Corman

How to Act and Eat at the Same Time by Tom Logan

How to Avoid the Cutting Room Floor by Jordan Goldman

How to Get Ideas by Jack Foster

Impro by Kenneth Johnstone

Improvisation for the Theater by Viola Spolin

Indie Film Producing: The Craft of Low Budget Filmmaking by Suzanne Lyons

It Would Be So Nice if You Weren't Here by Charles Grodin

Know Small Parts by Laura Cayouette

The Laws of Human Nature by Robert Greene

Live Cinema by Francis Ford Coppola

Love, Lucy by Lucille Ball

Making Movies by Sidney Lumet

Making Movies Work by Jon Boorstin

Meeting of Minds by Steve Allen

Movie Speak by Tony Bill

My Rendezvous with Life by Mary Pickford
Ogilvy on Advertising by David Ogilvy
100 Years, 100 Stories by George Burns
On Screen Acting by Edward and Jean Porter Dmytryk
A Pictorial History of the Silent Screen by Daniel Blum
The Pocket Muse by Monica Wood
The Power of Myth by Joseph Campbell
A Practical Handbook for the Actor by Melissa Bruder
Purple Cow by Seth Godin
Reading the Silver Screen by Thomas C. Foster
Sanford Meisner on Acting by Sanford Meisner
Stella Adler: The Art of Acting by Howard Kissel
Tips: Ideas for Actors by Jon Jory
True Strength by Kevin Sorbo
Understanding Movies by Louis Giannetti
Who is Michael Ovitz? by Michael Ovitz
Wild Bill Wellman: Hollywood Rebel by William Wellman Jr.

Mike Kimmel

About Susannah Devereux

Susannah Devereux was born in Alicante, Spain to an English mother and a father from New Zealand. Susannah's first intention was to be a dancer, but that changed after an accident. Drawing upon her dance background, however, Susannah became a successful model and did so for many years, predominantly working on fashion runways all over the world. She modeled throughout New Zealand and Australia, as well as London, Milan, and Los Angeles. Most notably, she became the bridal model for Colin Cole, New Zealand's premier fashion designer, for seven consecutive seasons.

Susannah left the fashion business to pursue her true calling and passion—acting—and went to study with Bryon Siron (who had trained with Stella Adler in New York) at the City Acting Studio in Sydney, Australia.

She returned to New Zealand to join the cast of **Shortland Street** in the recurring role of Diane Neilson. During her time back home, Susannah was invited to join a workshop set up by the New Zealand Film Commission with acting coach Jeremiah Comey from Los Angeles—a workshop for actors, writers and directors. There she met writer/director Jonathon Brough who wrote the film **The Model** for her. The film went on to be selected and screened at the Cannes Film Festival.

Susannah arrived in the United States in 1996, originally for a three-week vacation, but instantly fell in love with all that is America. She was granted a Green card as an Artist of Extraordinary Ability. Since her arrival in the U.S., she has appeared in numerous independent films working alongside the likes of Tim Meadows, Danny Trejo, John James, Robin Lively, W. Earl Brown, Richard Hatch, Robert Gossett and Jan Michael Vincent, along with television series including **The Wild Thornberrys** and, most recently, **Creepshow** alongside Academy nominee Bruce Davison. She has started producing film and web series in recent years. Susannah is always actively looking for interesting female-driven stories. She also embarked upon an entrepreneurial venture, establishing her own lifestyle brand in 2010—Devereux Bedding.

She now divides her time between Los Angeles, Atlanta, and Nashville.

About Mike Kimmel

Mike Kimmel is a film, television, stage, and commercial actor and acting coach. He is a twenty-plus year member of SAG-AFTRA with extensive experience in both the New York and Los Angeles markets. He has worked with directors Francis Ford Coppola, Robert Townsend, Craig Shapiro, and Christopher Cain among many others. TV credits include **Game of Silence**, **Zoo**, **Treme**, **In Plain Sight**, **Cold Case**, **Breakout Kings**, **Memphis Beat**, **Buffy The Vampire Slayer**, and **The Oprah Winfrey Show**. He was a regular sketch comedy player on **The Tonight Show**, performing live on stage and in pre-taped segments with Jay Leno for eleven years.

Mike has appeared in dozens of theatrical plays on both coasts, including Radio City Music Hall, Equity Library Theater, Stella Adler Theater, Double Image Theater, The Village Gate, and Theater at the Improv. He trained with Michael Shurtleff, William Hickey, Ralph Marrero, Gloria Maddox, Harold Sylvester, Wendy Davis, Amy Hunter, Bob Collier, and Stuart Robinson. He holds a B.A. from Brandeis University and an M.A. from California State University at Dominguez Hills.

He has taught at Upper Iowa University, University of New Orleans, University of Phoenix, Glendale Community College, Nunez Community College, Delgado Community College, and in the Los Angeles, Beverly Hills, and Burbank, California public school districts. He is a two-time past president of New Orleans Toastmasters, the public speaking organization.

Mike has written and collaborated on numerous scripts for stage and screen. ***In Lincoln's Footsteps***, his full-length historical drama on Presidents Lincoln and Garfield, was a semi-finalist in the National Playwrights Conference at the Eugene O'Neill Theater Center. Mike also received the Excellence in Teaching Award from Upper Iowa University in 2014.

Mike is a full voting member of the National Academy of Television Arts and Sciences, the organization that produces the Emmy Awards. He is the author of ***Scenes for Teens***, ***Acting Scenes for Kids and Tweens***, ***Monologues for Teens***, ***Monologues for Kids and Tweens***, ***One-Minute Monologues for Teens***, ***Monologues for Teens II***, ***Monologues for Kids and Tweens II***, and ***Six Critical Essays on Film: A College Guide for Film Appreciation***.

In 2019, the Independent Author Network selected Mike's third published book, ***Monologues for Teens***, as their Performing Arts Book of the Year. He is also featured and pictured in Francis Ford Coppola's groundbreaking 2017 book, ***Live Cinema***.

"For what it's worth: it's never too late to be whoever you want to be. I hope you live a life you're proud of, and if you find you're not, I hope you have the strength to start over."

~ F. Scott Fitzgerald

www.ingramcontent.com/pod-product-compliance
Lightning Source LLC
Chambersburg PA
CBHW072040110526
44592CB00012B/1492